ANDREW MURRAY

LIVING A
PRAYERFUL
LIFE

∾

Books by Andrew Murray

FROM BETHANY HOUSE PUBLISHERS

With Updated Language

Abiding in Christ

Absolute Surrender

The Andrew Murray Daily Reader

The Believer's Daily Renewal

Believing Prayer

The Blood of Christ

Divine Healing

The Fullness of the Spirit

Humility

A Life of Obedience

Living a Prayerful Life

The Ministry of Intercessory Prayer

The Path to Holiness

Teach Me to Pray

ANDREW MURRAY

LIVING A
PRAYERFUL
LIFE

❧

BETHANYHOUSE
Minneapolis, Minnesota

Living a Prayerful Life
Andrew Murray

Copyright © 1983, 2002
Bethany House Publishers

Newly edited and updated for today's reader by Nancy Renich.
Formerly published under the titles *The Prayer Life* and *The Believer's Prayer Life*.

Cover design by Cheryl Neisen

Published by Bethany House Publishers
11400 Hampshire Avenue South
Bloomington, Minnesota 55438

Bethany House Publishers is a division of
Baker Publishing Group, Grand Rapids, Michigan.

Printed in the United States of America

Library of Congress Cataloging-in-Publication Data

Murray, Andrew, 1828–1917.
    [Prayer life]
    Living a prayerful life : a classic devotional edited for today's reader / by Andrew Murray.
        p. cm.
Originally published: The prayer life ; The believer's life. Minneapolis, Minn. : Bethany House, 1983.
    ISBN 0-7642-2715-7 (pbk.)
    1. Prayer—Christianity. I. Title.
    BV210.3 .M86   2002
    248.3'2—dc21   2002010732

ANDREW MURRAY was born in South Africa in 1828. After receiving his education in Scotland and Holland, he returned to Africa and spent many years as a missionary pastor. He and his wife, Emma, raised eight children. He is best known for his many devotional books, including some of the most enduring classics of Christian literature.

Introduction

Knowing the origin of this book and the reason why it was written will help the reader better understand its teaching.

It came out of a ministers' conference at Stellenbosch, South Africa, April 11–14, 1912. Professor de Vos, of our Dutch Reformed Theological Seminary, had written a letter to our church ministers concerning the low spiritual state that marked the church in general and which ought to lead us to inquire how far the statement included our church as well. What was said about the lack of spiritual power in the book *The State of the Church* called for deep searching of the heart, since Professor de Vos thought the statement was true. He suggested we come together and in God's presence find the cause of the lack. He wrote: "If we but study the conditions in all sincerity, we will have to acknowledge that our unbelief and our sins are the cause of our lack of spiritual power, and that this condition is one that places us guilty before God and grieving God's Holy Spirit."

His invitation met with a hearty response. Our four theological professors, together with more than two hundred ministers, missionaries, and theological students, met on the basis of the above statement as the keynote of our meeting. From the very first message, there was a tone of confession as the only way to repentance and restoration. Then opportunity was given for testimony as to what the sins might be that made the life of the church so ineffectual. Some began to mention failures in conduct, in presentation of doctrine, or in service that they had seen in other ministers. Soon it was felt that this was not the right approach; each must acknowledge his personal guilt.

The Lord led us gradually to the sin of prayerlessness as one of the deepest roots of the problem. No one could claim to be free from this. Nothing so reveals a defective spiritual life in a minister or a congregation as the lack of believing and unceasing prayer. Prayer is the pulse of the spiritual life. It is the great means by which ministers and laypeople alike receive the blessing and power of heaven. Persevering and believing prayer precludes a strong and abundant life.

When the spirit of confession began to prevail, the question came up as to whether it would be possible to gain victory over all that had in the past hindered our prayer life. In smaller sessions held previously, many had been anxious to make a new beginning and yet doubted that they would be able to maintain a prayer life consistent with what they saw in the Word of God. Though they often made the attempt, they had utterly failed. They did not dare to promise the Lord that they would live and pray as He would have them do, because they felt such a thing was impossible. Such confessions gradually led to the revelation that the only power to be found for a new prayer life was in an entirely new relationship to the Savior. As we see in Him the Lord who saves us from sin—even the sin of prayerlessness—our faith yields itself to a life of closer intimacy with Him. Then a life in His love and fellowship will make prayer the natural expression of our inner life. Before we parted, many testified that they were returning with new light and new hope of finding in Jesus Christ strength for a renewed prayer life.

Many felt that this was only the beginning. Satan, who had so long prevailed in the place of prayer, would do his utmost again to tempt us to yield to the power of the flesh and the world. Nothing but the teaching and fellowship of Christ himself could give power to remain faithful.

The need was expressed for a statement of the truths dealt with at the conference to remind those present of what they had learned and what might help them in their new endeavor after the prayer life so essential to a minister's success. It was also needed for those who were not able to attend, and for the church elders, who had in many cases had a deep interest in hearing the purpose for which their ministers had gathered.

Early copies of the book were sent out with the thought that if the leaders of the church could see that in spiritual work *everything depends upon prayer,* and that God himself helps those who wait on Him, it could truly be a day of hope for our church. It was also intended for all believers who longed for a life of complete separation to the Lord. For all who desired to pray more and pray more effectively, it pointed to the glory of God in the personal place of prayer and the way that power can rest upon the soul.

When first asked to have the book translated into English, I felt that its composition had been too hurried and its tone, because of the close connection with the meetings that had preceded these, too colloquial to make it desirable. My own limited strength made it impossible for me to think of rewriting it. When, however, my friend the Rev. W. M. Douglas asked permission to translate it, I consented. If God has a message through the book to any of His servants, I would count it a privilege to tell what He has done here in our church as an encouragement for what He might do in other churches.

I close with my greetings to all ministers of the gospel and church members who may read these pages. The grace of God has wrought among us conviction of sin, confession of deep need and helplessness, and then given us the vision and the faith for what Jesus Christ can do for those who fully trust Him. I pray that He will also give many who read these pages the courage to meet with their co-workers and to seek for and obtain that full fellowship with God in prayer that is the very essence of the Christian life. It has been said, "Only the prayerless are too proud to own up to prayerlessness." Let us believe that many hearts are waiting for the call inviting them to united and wholehearted confession of sin as the only way to a return and restoration of God's favor and the experience of answers to prayer.

I wish to add one more word in regard to the Pentecostal prayer meetings held throughout our church. These have had an interesting and important place in our work. At the time of the great revival in America and Ireland in 1858, and the years following, some of our elder ministers issued a circular urging the churches to pray that God might visit us too. In 1860 revival broke out in various parishes. And in April 1861 there was a deep interest shown in this practice of prayer in one of our oldest congregations. During the week preceding Pentecost Sunday, the minister, who ordinarily preached only once on a Sunday, announced that there would be a public prayer meeting in the church in the afternoon. The occasion was one of extraordinary interest, and many hearts were deeply touched. One result was that the minister suggested that the ten days between Ascension and Pentecost Sunday should be observed by daily prayer meetings. This took place the following year. Such blessing was received that all the neighboring congregations adopted the idea, and now for fifty years these ten days of prayer have been observed throughout the whole church. Each year notes were distributed outlining the subjects of the messages and prayer. As a result, Christians throughout our whole church have been educated in the knowledge of what God's Word teaches regarding the Holy Spirit, and have been stirred to seek His blessed leading and yield themselves to it. These ten days have often led to special effort with the unconverted and the beginnings of revival. They have been the means of untold blessing in leading ministers and people to recognize the place that the Holy Spirit ought to have as the executive of the Godhead in the heart of believers, in dealing with souls, and in consecration to the service of the kingdom. Much is still lacking of the full knowledge and power of the Holy Spirit, but we feel that we cannot be sufficiently grateful to God for what He has done through leading us to dedicate these days to special prayer for His Holy Spirit to work.

I have written about this with the thought that some will not only be glad to know of it but they also will unite in the same observance in their congregations.

—Andrew Murray

Contents

Part One

The Prayer Life

Chapter 1

The Sin of Prayerlessness

If conscience is to do its work and the contrite heart is to feel its proper remorse, it is necessary for each individual to confess his sin by name. The confession must be intensely personal. In a meeting of ministers, probably no single sin should be acknowledged with deeper shame than the sin of prayerlessness. Each one of us needs to confess that we are guilty of this.

Why is prayerlessness such a serious sin? At first it would seem to be merely a weakness. So much is said about lack of time and all sorts of distractions that the deep guilt of the situation is not recognized. From now on, let us acknowledge prayerlessness as the sin that it is.

1. *It is a reproach to God.* The holy and most glorious God invites us to come to Him, to converse with Him, to ask Him for the things we need, and to experience the depth of blessing there is in fellowship with Him. He has created us in His own image and has redeemed us by His own Son, so that in conversation with Him we should find our greatest delight.

What use do we make of this heavenly privilege? How many of us admit to taking a mere five minutes for prayer! The claim is that there is no time. The reality is that a heart desire for prayer is lacking. Many do not know how to spend half an hour with God! It is not that they absolutely do not pray; they may pray every day—but they have no joy in prayer. Joy is the sign that God is everything to you.

If a friend comes to visit, there is time. We make time—even at the cost of something else—for the sake of enjoying pleasant conversation with our friend. Yes, there is time for everything that truly interests us, but time is scarce to practice fellowship with God and to enjoy being with Him! We find time for someone who can be of service to us; but day after day, month after month passes, and for many there is no time to spend even one hour with God.

We must acknowledge that we disrespect and dishonor God when we say we cannot find time for fellowship with Him. If this sin begins to appear ordinary to us, we must cry out to God: "O God, be merciful to me, and forgive me this awful sin of prayerlessness."

2. *It is the cause of a deficient spiritual life.* Prayerlessness is proof that for the most part our life is still under the power of the flesh. Prayer is the pulse of life; by it the doctor can diagnose the condition of the heart. The sin of prayerlessness proves to the ordinary Christian or minister that the life of God in the soul is mortally sick and weak.

Much is said and many complaints are made about the failure of the church to fulfill her calling, to exercise an influence on her members, to deliver them from the power of the world, and to bring them to a life of holy consecration to God. Much is also said about the church's indifference to the millions for whom Christ died who depend upon her to make known to them His love and salvation. Why is it that thousands of Christian workers in the world have no greater influence than they do? I venture to say that it is because of prayerlessness. With all their zeal for study and work in the church, in spite of all their faithfulness in preaching and encouragement of the people, they lack the prayer that brings the Spirit and power from on high. The sin of prayerlessness is the root cause of a powerless spiritual life.

3. *The church suffers great loss as a result of the prayerlessness of their minister.* A minister's business is to train believers for a life of prayer. How can a leader do this if he himself understands little about the art of conversing with God and of receiving from the Holy Spirit each day abundant grace for himself and for his work? A minister cannot lead a congregation higher than he is himself. He cannot with enthusiasm point out a way or explain a work in which he himself neither walks nor lives.

How many thousands of Christians know next to nothing of the blessedness of prayer fellowship with God! How many know something of it and long to know more, but the preaching of the Word does not urge it of its hearers. The reason is no doubt that the minister understands little about the secret of powerful prayer himself, and so does not give it the place in his service that in the nature of the case and in the will of God is indispensably necessary. What a difference we would notice in our congregations if ministers could see the sin of prayerlessness in its proper light and be delivered from it!

4. *It is impossible to preach the gospel to all men—as we are commanded by Christ to do—as long as this sin is not acknowledged and dealt with.* Many feel that the greatest need of missions is finding men and women who will give themselves to the Lord for the salvation of souls. It has also been said that God is eager and able to deliver and bless the world He has redeemed if His people are willing and ready to cry

to Him day and night. But how can congregations be brought to that place without our ministers recognizing that the indispensable thing is not preaching, pastoral visitation, or church activity, but fellowship with God in prayer?

Oh, that all thought and work and expectation concerning the kingdom might drive us to the acknowledgment of prayerlessness as sin! *God, help us to see it! Deliver us from it through the blood and power of Jesus! Teach every minister of the Word what a glorious place he can occupy if he is first delivered from his lack of prayer, so that with courage and joy, in faith and perseverance, he can go on with God.*

May the Lord lay the burden of the sin of prayerlessness so heavy on our hearts that we may not rest until it is taken far from us through the name and power of Jesus.

A Witness From America

In 1898 two members of the presbytery of New York attended the Northfield Conference for the deepening of the spiritual life. They returned to their work with the fire of a new enthusiasm as they endeavored to bring about a revival in the entire presbytery. In a meeting they held, the chairman was led to ask the group about their prayer life: "Brethren," he said, "let us today make confession before God and each other. It will do us good. Will everyone who spends half an hour each day with God in connection with His work, raise your hand?" One hand was raised. He made a further request: "All who spend fifteen minutes in this way, raise your hand." Less than half of the hands went up. Then he said, "Prayer is the working power of the church of Christ, and half of the workers make hardly any use of it! All who spend five minutes a day hold up your hand." All hands went up, but one man came later with the confession that he was not sure if he spent five minutes in prayer every day. "It is," said he, "a terrible revelation of how little time I spend with God."

Chapter 2

The Cause of Prayerlessness

In an elders' prayer meeting, one brother asked: "What is the cause of so much prayerlessness? Is it unbelief?"

The answer was: "Certainly; but what is the cause of unbelief?" The disciples asked the Lord Jesus: "Why could we not cast the devil out?" His answer was: "Because of your unbelief." He added: "Howbeit, this kind goes out only by prayer and fasting." If the life is not one of self-denial—of fasting (letting the world go) and of prayer (laying hold of heaven)—faith cannot be exercised. In a life lived according to the flesh and not according to the Spirit, we find the origin of the prayerlessness of which we complain. As we left the meeting, one brother said to me, "The whole difficulty is that we wish to pray in the Spirit and at the same time walk after the flesh. This is impossible."

If one is sick and desires healing, it is of prime importance that the true cause of the sickness be discovered. This is always the first step toward recovery. If the root problem is not recognized, and attention is directed toward the wrong cause or to secondary problems, healing is out of the question. In like manner, it is of utmost importance for us to obtain correct insight into the cause of the sad condition of deadness and failure in our private place of prayer, which should be a blessed place. Let us seek to fully recognize the root of this problem.

Scripture teaches us that there are only two conditions possible for the Christian: one is to walk according to the Spirit and the other is to walk according the flesh. These two powers are in irreconcilable conflict with each other. So most Christians—even though they may be born again through the Spirit and have received the life of God—still continue to live their life not according to the Spirit but according to the flesh. Paul wrote to the Galatians: "Are you so foolish? After beginning with the Spirit, are you now trying to attain your goal by human effort?" (Galatians 3:3). Their service lay in fleshly outward performances. They did not understand that where the flesh is permitted to influence service to God, it soon results in open sin.

So he mentions as the work of the flesh not only grave sins such as adultery, murder, and drunkenness but also the more ordinary sins of daily life: anger, strife, and arguing. Then he exhorts: "Live by the Spirit, and you will not gratify the desires of the sinful nature. . . . Since we live by the Spirit, let us keep in step with the Spirit" (Galatians 5:16, 25). The Spirit must be honored not only as the author of a new life but also as the leader and director of our entire walk. Otherwise we are what the apostle calls "carnal" or fleshly.

The majority of Christians have little understanding in this matter. They have no real knowledge of the deep sinfulness and godlessness of the carnal nature to which they unconsciously yield. "God . . . condemned sin in sinful man" (Romans 8:3)—through the cross of Christ. "Those who belong to Christ Jesus have crucified the sinful nature with its passions and desires" (Galatians 5:24). The flesh cannot be improved or sanctified. "The sinful mind is hostile to God. It does not submit to God's law, nor can it do so" (Romans 8:7). There is no means of dealing with the flesh except as Christ dealt with it, bearing it to the cross. "We know that our old self was crucified with him" (Romans 6:6); so we by faith also crucify it and regard it and treat it daily as a cursed thing that finds its rightful place on the cross.

It is unfortunate that so many Christians seldom think or speak seriously about the deep and immeasurable sinfulness of the flesh. Paul said, "I know that nothing good lives in me, that is, in my sinful nature" (Romans 7:18). The man who truly believes this may well cry out: "I see another law at work in the members of my body.... What a wretched man I am! Who will rescue me from this body of death?" (Romans 7:23–24). Happy is the one who can go a step further and say: "Thanks be to God—through Jesus Christ our Lord! ... Through Christ Jesus the law of the spirit of life set me free from the law of sin and death" (Romans 7:25; 8:2).

Oh, that we would understand God's supreme grace toward us: The flesh was put on the cross; the Spirit dwells in the heart and controls the life.

This spiritual life is too little understood or sought after; yet it is literally what God has promised and will accomplish in those who unconditionally surrender themselves to Him for this purpose.

Here, then, we see this deep root of sin as the cause of the prayerless life. The flesh can say prayers well enough, calling itself religious for so doing, and thus satisfy the conscience. But the flesh has no desire or strength for the prayer that strives after an intimate knowledge of God, that rejoices in fellowship with Him, and that continues to lay hold of His strength. So, finally, it comes to this: the flesh must be denied and crucified.

The Christian who is still carnal (fleshly) has neither the disposition nor the strength to follow after God. He remains satisfied with his prayer of habit or custom. But the glory and the blessedness of secret prayer is a hidden thing to him, until one day his eyes are opened, and he begins to see that the flesh in its disposition to turn away from God is the arch-enemy that makes powerful prayer impossible.

At a conference I spoke on the subject of prayer and used strong words about the enmity of the flesh as a cause of prayerlessness. After my talk, the minister's wife said that she thought I had spoken too strongly. She also regretted that she had too little desire for prayer, but she knew her heart was sincerely set on seeking God. I showed her what the Word of God said about the flesh, and that everything that prevents the reception of the Spirit is a secret work of the flesh. Adam was created to have fellowship with God and enjoyed it before his fall. But after the Fall, immediately there came a deep-seated aversion to God, and Adam fled from Him. This incurable aversion is characteristic of the unregenerate nature and the chief cause of our unwillingness to surrender ourselves to fellowship with God in prayer. The following day that woman told me that God had opened her eyes. She confessed that the enmity and unwillingness of the flesh was the hidden hindrance in her defective prayer life.

Do not seek to find in circumstances the explanation for this prayerlessness over which we mourn. Seek it where God's Word declares it to be—in the hidden aversion of the heart to a holy God.

When a Christian does not yield completely to the leading of the Spirit—and such a surrender is certainly the will of God and the work of His grace—he lives, without knowing it, under the power of the flesh. This life in the flesh manifests itself in many different ways. It appears

- in the hastiness of spirit or the anger that so unexpectedly arises in you;
- in the lack of love for which you have so often blamed yourself;
- in the over-pleasure found in eating and drinking, about which at times your conscience has chided you;
- in seeking after your own will and honor, confidence in your own wisdom and power, and pleasure in the world, of which you are sometimes ashamed before God.

All this is life "after the flesh." "You are still worldly" (1 Corinthians 3:3). If there is strife or quarreling among us, we are still worldly. Perhaps this text disturbs you at times; you do not have full peace and joy in God.

Take time to answer the question: "Have I found here the cause of my prayerlessness, of my powerlessness to effect any change in the matter? I live in the Spirit; I have been born again, but I do not walk after the Spirit—the flesh rules over me. The carnal (fleshly) life cannot possibly pray in the spirit with power. God forgive me. My carnal life is obviously the cause of my shameful prayerlessness.

The Storm Center on the Battlefield

Mention was made in a conference of the expression "strategic position," used so often in reference to the great strife between the kingdom of heaven and the powers of darkness.

When a general chooses the place from which he intends to strike his enemy, he pays most attention to those points that he thinks most important in the fight. On the battlefield of Waterloo, there was a farmhouse that Wellington immediately saw as the key to the situation. He did not spare his troops in his endeavor to hold that point: the victory depended on it. And so it happened as he predicted it would. It is the same in the conflict between the believer and the powers of darkness. The place of private prayer is the key, the strategic position, where decisive victory is obtained.

The Enemy uses all his power to lead the Christian—and above all, the minister—to neglect prayer. Satan knows that however admirable the sermon may be, however attractive the service, however faithful the pastoral visitation, none of these things can damage him or his kingdom if prayer is neglected. When the church closes herself in to the power of the prayer meeting, and the soldiers of the Lord have received on their knees "power from on High," then the powers of darkness will be shaken and souls will be delivered. In the church, on the mission field, with the minister and his congregation, everything depends on the faithful exercise of prayer.

During the week of conference, I found the following illustration in *The Christian*:

> Two persons quarrel over a certain point. We call them Christian and Apollyon. Apollyon notices that Christian has a certain weapon that would give him a sure victory. They meet in deadly strife, and Apollyon resolves to take away the weapon from his opponent and destroy it. For the moment, the main cause of the strife has become subordinate to: who will gain possession of the weapon on which

everything depends? It is of vital importance to get hold of it.

So it is in the conflict between Satan and the believer. God's child can conquer anything and everything by prayer. Is it any wonder that Satan does his utmost to snatch that weapon from the Christian or hinder him in the use of it?

How does Satan stand in the way of prayer? He hinders it by the temptation to postpone or curtail it; by bringing in wandering thoughts and all sorts of distractions; and through unbelief and hopelessness. Happy is the prayer hero who, through it all, takes care to hold fast to his weapon and use it regularly. Like our Lord in Gethsemane, the more violently the Enemy attacked, the more earnestly He prayed, and He did not stop until He had obtained the victory. After naming all the other parts of the armor, Paul adds, "And pray in the Spirit on all occasions with all kinds of prayers and requests. With this in mind, be alert and always keep on praying for all the saints" (Ephesians 6:18). Without prayer, the helmet of salvation, the shield of faith, and the Sword of the Spirit (God's Word) have no power. All depend on prayer. *God, teach us to believe and hold fast to prayer!*

Chapter 3

The Fight Against Prayerlessness

As soon as the Christian becomes convinced of his sin in this matter, his first thought is that he must begin to strive, with God's help, to gain the victory over it. But soon he finds that his striving is worth little. The discouraging thought comes over him: he cannot continue faithful! At conferences on the subject of prayer during the past years, many a minister has said openly that it seemed impossible for him to attain to such a strict life.

Recently I received a letter from a minister well known for his ability and devotion:

> As far as I am concerned, it does not seem to help me to hear too much about the life of prayer, about the strenuous exertion for which we must prepare ourselves, and about all the time and trouble and endless effort it will cost us. These things discourage me—I have heard them so often. Time after time I have put them to the test, and the result has always been sadly disappointing. It does not help me to be told: "You must pray more, and hold a closer watch over yourself, and become altogether a more earnest Christian."

My reply to him was as follows: "I think in all I said at the conference or elsewhere, I have never mentioned exertion or struggle, because I am so entirely convinced that our efforts are futile unless we first learn how to abide in Christ by a simple faith."

My correspondent said further: "The message I need is this: 'See that your relationship to your living Savior is what it ought to be. Live in His presence, rejoice in His love, rest in Him.'" A better message could not be given, if it is only rightly understood. *See that your relationship to the living Savior is what it ought to be.* But this is exactly what will make it possible for you to live the life of prayer.

We must not comfort ourselves with thoughts of standing in a right relationship to the Lord Jesus while the sin of prayerlessness has any power over us and while we, along with the whole church, complain about our weak life that makes us unfit to pray for ourselves, for the church, or for missions as we should. But if we first recognize that a right relationship to the Lord Jesus above all else includes prayer, with both the desire and power to pray according to God's will, then we have something that gives us the right to rejoice in Him and to rest in Him.

This incident points out how naturally discouragement is the result of self-effort, and so blocks out all hope of improvement or victory. Indeed, this is the condition of many Christians when called on to persevere in prayer as intercessors. They feel it is something entirely beyond their reach: they do not have the power for the self-sacrifice and consecration necessary for such prayer. And they shrink from the effort and struggle that will, they assume, make them unhappy. They have tried in the power of the flesh to conquer the flesh—a wholly impossible thing. They have endeavored by Beelzebub to cast out Beelzebub—and this will never happen. It is Jesus alone who can subdue the flesh and the devil.

We have spoken of a struggle that will certainly result in disappointment and discouragement. This is the effort made in our own strength. But there is another struggle that will certainly lead to victory. The Scripture speaks of "the good fight of faith," that is to say, a fight that springs from and is carried on by faith. We must secure a right concept of faith and stand fast in our faith. Jesus Christ is the author and finisher of faith. When we come into right relationship with Him, we can be sure of His help and power. Just as earnestly as we must in the first place say, "Do not strive in your own strength. Cast yourself at the feet of the Lord Jesus and wait upon Him in the sure confidence that He is with you and works in you"; so do we in the second place say, "Strive in prayer; let faith fill your heart—so will you be strong in the Lord and in the power of His might."

An illustration will help us to understand this: A devoted Christian woman who conducted a large Bible class with zeal and success, once came troubled to her minister. In her earlier years she had enjoyed much blessing in her place of private prayer, in fellowship with the Lord, and in His Word. But this fellowship had gradually been lost, and whatever she did, she could not regain it. The Lord had blessed her work, but the joy had gone out of her life. The minister asked what she had done to regain the lost blessing. "I have done everything that I could think of," she said, "but all was in vain."

He then questioned her about her experience in connection with her conversion. She gave an immediate and clear answer: "At first I spared no pains in my attempt to become better and to free myself from sin, but it was all useless. At last I began to understand that I must lay aside all my efforts and simply trust the Lord Jesus to bestow on me His life and peace; and He did it."

"Why, then," said the minister, "do you not try this again? As you go to pray, however cold and dark your heart may be, do not try in your own might to force yourself into the right attitude. Bow before Him and tell Him that He sees in what a poor state you are and that your only hope is in Him. Trust Him with a childlike trust to have mercy upon you and then wait upon Him. With such trust you are in a right relationship to Him. You have nothing; He has everything." Some time later she told the minister that his advice had helped her; she had learned that faith in the love of the Lord Jesus is the only method for getting into fellowship with God in prayer.

Do you see that there are two kinds of warfare? The first is when we seek to conquer prayerlessness in our own strength. In that case my advice to you is: "Give up your restlessness and effort; fall helpless at the feet of the Lord Jesus; He will speak the word, and your soul will live." If you have done this, I give you the second message: "This is only the beginning. It will require deep earnestness, the exercise of all your power, and a watchfulness of the entire heart— eager to detect the least backsliding. Above all, it will require surrender to a life of self-sacrifice, which God desires to see in us and that He will work out for us."

Chapter 4

How to Be Delivered From Prayerlessness

The greatest stumbling block in the way of victory over prayerlessness is the secret feeling that we will never obtain the blessing of being delivered from it. Often we have tried, but in vain. Old habits, the power of the flesh, and our surroundings with their varied attractions and distractions, have been too strong for us. What good does it do to attempt what our heart assures us is out of our reach? The change needed in the entire life is too great and too difficult. If the question is put: "Is a change possible?" our sighing heart says, "For me it is entirely *im*possible!" Do you know why we answer like that? It is simply because we have heard the call to prayer as the voice of Moses and as a command of the law. Moses and his law have never given anyone the power to obey.

Do you really long for the courage to believe that deliverance from a prayerless life is possible for you and may become a reality? Then you must learn the great lesson that such a deliverance is included in the redemption that is in Christ Jesus, that it is one of the blessings of the new covenant that God himself will impart to you through Christ Jesus. As you begin to understand this, you will find that the exhortation "Pray without ceasing" conveys a new meaning. Hope begins to spring up in your heart that the Spirit—who has been bestowed on you to cry constantly, "Abba, Father"—will make a true life of prayer possible for you. Then you will hearken not in the spirit of discouragement but in the gladness of hope to the voice that calls you to repentance.

Many a person has turned to his place of prayer under bitter self-accusation that he has prayed so little, and he has resolved for the future to live in a different manner. Yet no blessing has come—there has not been the strength to continue faithful, and the call to repentance has had no power because his eyes were not fixed on the Lord Jesus. If he had only understood, he would have said, "Lord, you see how cold and dark my heart is. I know that I must pray, but I feel I cannot do so. I lack the urgency and desire to pray."

He did not know that at that same moment the Lord Jesus in His tender love was looking down upon him and saying, "You cannot pray. You feel that all is cold and dark. Why not give yourself over into my hands? Only believe that I am ready to help you in prayer. I long to pour my love into your heart so that you, in the consciousness of weakness, may confidently rely on me to bestow the grace of prayer. Just as I will cleanse you from all other sins, so also will I deliver you from the sin of prayerlessness—only do not seek the victory in your own strength. Bow before me as one who expects everything from his Savior. Let your soul keep silence before me, however lame you feel your state is. Be assured of this: I will teach you how to pray."

Many will acknowledge: "I see my mistake. I had not

thought that the Lord Jesus must deliver and cleanse me from this sin also. I had not understood that He was with me every day as I prayed, ready in His great love to keep and to bless me, however sinful and guilty I felt myself to be. I had not supposed that just as He will give all other grace in answer to prayer, so, first and most of all, He will bestow the grace of a praying heart. What folly to think that all other blessings must come from Him, but that prayer, on which everything else depends, must be obtained by personal effort! Thank God, I have begun to comprehend: The Lord Jesus himself is in my prayer closet, watching over me and holding himself responsible to teach me how to approach the Father. He only asks that I, with childlike confidence, wait upon Him and glorify Him.

Have we forgotten this truth? From a defective spiritual life, nothing better can be expected than a defective prayer life. It is vain for us to endeavor to pray more or better while we remain in a state of spiritual drought. *It is an impossibility.* It is essential that we experience that "he who is in Christ Jesus is a new creature: old things have passed away; behold, all things are become new." This is literally true for the man who understands and experiences what it is to be in Christ.

Our whole relationship to the Lord Jesus must be a new thing. I must believe in His infinite love, which longs to have communion with me every moment and to keep me in the enjoyment of His fellowship. I must believe in His divine power, which has conquered sin and will truly keep me from it. I must believe in Him who, as the great Intercessor, through the Spirit, will inspire each member of His body with joy and power for communion with God in prayer. My prayer life must be brought entirely under the control of Christ and His love. Then for the first time prayer will become what it really is: the natural and joyous breathing of the spiritual life, by which the heavenly atmosphere is inhaled and then exhaled in prayer.

Do you see that when this faith possesses us, the call to a life of prayer that pleases God will be a welcome call? The cry "Repent of the sin of prayerlessness" will not be responded to by a sigh of helplessness or by the unwillingness of the flesh. The voice of the Father will be heard as He sets before us a widely opened door and receives us into blessed fellowship with himself. Prayer for the Spirit's help to pray will no longer be in fear of an effort too great for our own power. Instead, it will be merely falling down in utter weakness at the feet of the Lord Jesus to find there that victory comes through the might and love that stream from His countenance.

Perhaps the question arises in our mind: *Will this continue?* Fear follows, "You know how often you have tried and been disappointed." But now faith finds strength, not in the thought of what you will do, but in the changeless faithfulness and love of Christ, who once again helps and assures you that those who wait on Him shall not be ashamed.

If fear and hesitation still remain, I pray that you by the mercies of God in Jesus Christ and by the unspeakable faithfulness of His tender love, dare to cast yourselves at His feet. Only believe with your whole heart—there is deliverance from the sin of prayerlessness. "If we confess our sins, he is faithful and just and will forgive us our sins and purify us from all unrighteousness" (1 John 1:9). In His blood and grace there is complete deliverance from all unrighteousness and from all prayerlessness. Praise His name forever!

Chapter 5

How Deliverance From Prayerlessness Might Continue

What we have said about deliverance from the sin of prayerlessness also applies to answer the question "How may the experience of deliverance be maintained?" Redemption is not granted to us piecemeal, as something of which we may use a part from time to time. It is bestowed as a fullness of grace stored up in the Lord Jesus, which may be enjoyed in new fellowship with Him every day. It is so necessary that this great truth be driven home and fixed in our minds that I will say it again: Nothing can preserve you from carelessness or make it possible for you to persevere in living, powerful prayer, except daily close fellowship with Jesus our Lord.

He said to His disciples: "Trust in God; trust also in me. . . . Believe me when I say that I am in the Father and the Father is in me. . . . Anyone who has faith in me will do what I have been doing. He will even do greater things than these, because I am going to the Father" (John 14:1, 11–12).

The Lord wanted to teach His disciples that all they had

learned from the Old Testament concerning the power and holiness and love of God must now be transferred to Him. They must not believe merely in certain written documents but in Him personally. They must believe that He was in the Father, and the Father in Him, in such a sense that they had one life and one glory. All they knew about God they would find in Christ. He laid great emphasis on this, because it was only through such faith in Him and His divine glory that they could do the works that He did, and even greater works. This faith would lead them to know that just as Christ and the Father are one, so also they were in Christ, and Christ was in them.

It is this intimate, spiritual, personal, uninterrupted relationship to the Lord Jesus that manifests itself powerfully in our lives, and especially in our prayer lives. All the glorious attributes of God are in our Lord Jesus Christ. What does this mean?

1. *God's omnipresence* with which He fills the world and every moment is present in everything. Like the Father, so now our Lord Jesus is everywhere present, above all with each of His redeemed ones. This is one of the greatest and most important lessons our faith must grasp. We can clearly understand this from the example of our Lord's disciples. What was the peculiar privilege of these disciples who were always in fellowship with Him? It was uninterrupted enjoyment of the presence of the Lord Jesus. Because of this they were extremely sorrowful at the thought of His death. They would be deprived of that presence; He would be with them no longer. Under these circumstances, how did the Lord Jesus comfort them? He promised that the Holy Spirit from heaven should work in them such a sense of the fullness of His life and of His personal presence that He would be even

more intimately near and have more unbroken fellowship with them than they experienced while He was on the earth.

This great promise is now the inheritance of every believer, although so many know little about it. Jesus Christ, in His divine personality, in that eternal love that led Him to the cross, longs to have fellowship with us every moment of the day and to keep us in the enjoyment of that fellowship. This ought to be explained to every new convert: "The Lord loves you so much that He would have you near Him without a break so that you may experience His love." Every believer who has felt his powerlessness for a life of prayer, of obedience, and of holiness must learn this. This alone will give us power as intercessors to conquer the world and to win souls for our Lord.

2. *The omnipotence of God.* God's power is wonderful! We see it in creation; we see it in the wonders of redemption recorded in the Old Testament. We see it in the wonderful works of Christ that the Father wrought in Him, and above all, in Christ's resurrection from the dead. We are called on to believe in the Son just as we believe in the Father. Yes, the Lord Jesus, who in His love is so unspeakably near us, is the Almighty One with whom nothing is impossible. Whatever may be in our hearts or flesh that will not bow to His will, He can and will conquer. Everything that is promised in God's Word, and all that is our inheritance as children of the new covenant, the almighty Jesus can bestow upon us. When I bow before Him in prayer, I am in contact with the eternal, unchanging power of God. When I commit myself for the day to the Lord Jesus, I may rest assured that His eternal, almighty power takes me under its protection and accomplishes everything for me.

If only we would take time for the hidden place of prayer,

so that we might experience in full the presence of Jesus! What a blessed life would be ours through faith—an unbroken fellowship with an omnipresent and almighty Lord.

3. *The holy love of God.* This means that with His whole heart He offers all His divine attributes for our service and is prepared to impart himself to us. Christ is the full revelation of God's love. He is the Son of that love—the gift of His love—the power of His love. This Jesus, who on the cross gave overwhelming proof of His love by His death and the shedding of His blood so as to make it impossible for us not to believe in that love, is He who comes to meet us in the place of private prayer. There He gives positive assurance of unbroken fellowship with Him as our inheritance. Through Him it will become our experience. The holy love of God that sacrificed everything to conquer sin and bring it to nothing comes to us in Christ to save us from sin.

Think about our Lord's words: "Believe me when I say that I am in the Father and the Father is in me. [And] you know him, for he lives with you and will be in you" (John 14:11, 17). Those words are the secret of the life of prayer. Take time in your place of prayer to bow down and worship. Wait on Him until He reveals himself, takes possession of you, and goes with you to show you how a person may live and walk in abiding fellowship with Him.

Do you long to know how you may always experience deliverance from the sin of prayerlessness? Here you have the secret. Believe in the Son of God; give Him time in your quiet place of prayer to reveal himself in His ever-present nearness as the Eternal, Almighty One, the Eternal Love who watches over you. Then you will experience something that you possibly have not known before: It has not entered into the heart of man what God can do for those who love Him.

Chapter 6

The Blessing of Victory

If we are delivered from the sin of prayerlessness and understand how this deliverance may continue to be experienced, what will be the fruit of our liberty? He who grasps this truth will seek after this freedom with renewed enthusiasm and perseverance. His life and experience will show that he has obtained something of unspeakable worth. He will be a living witness of the blessing found in victory.

1. *The blessedness of unbroken fellowship with God.* Think of the confidence in the Father that will replace the reproach and self-condemnation that characterized our lives before. Think of the deep consciousness we will have that God's almighty grace has effected something in us, proving that we bear His image and are fitted for a life of communion with Him. In spite of the conviction of our own unworthiness, think how we may live as children of the King in communion with our Father, and how we may manifest something of the character of our Lord Jesus that He had when He was on earth. Think how the hour of prayer may become the happiest time in our whole day, and how God may use us there to share in carrying out His plans, making us a fountain of blessing to the world around us.

2. *The power we may have for the work to which we are*

called. The preacher will learn to receive his message from God through the power of the Holy Spirit and to deliver it in that power to his congregation. He will know where he can be filled with the love and zeal that will enable him in his pastoral visiting to meet and help each individual in a spirit of compassion. He will be able to say with Paul: "I can do all things through Christ who strengthens me." We are more than conquerors through him that loved us. We are ambassadors for Christ, calling all men to be reconciled to God. These are not dreams or pictures of a vain imagination. God has given Paul as an example, so that though we may differ from him in our gifts or calling, by experience we may know the all-sufficiency of grace that can do all things for us as it did for him.

3. *The prospect that opens before us the future:* to be consecrated as intercessors in the work of bearing in our hearts the needs of the entire church and of the world. Paul sought to stir men to pray for all the saints, and he tells us what a burden he had for those who had not yet seen his face. In his personal presence he was subject to conditions of time and place, but in the Spirit he had power in the name of Christ to pray for blessing on those who had not yet heard of the Savior. In addition to his life in connection with men here on earth, near or far, he lived another life—one of love and of power in prayer, which he continually exercised. We can hardly conceive of the power God will bestow when we are freed from the sin of prayerlessness and pray with the boldness that reaches heaven in the almighty name of Christ to bring down blessing.

What a prospect! Ministers and missionaries brought by God's grace to pray with full faith and joy! What a difference it would make in our preaching, in our prayer meetings, in our fellowship with others! What power would fall in a prayer room, sanctified by communion with God and His love through Christ. What influence would be exercised on believers, urging them forward in the work of intercession. How great this influence would be felt throughout the church and among the unsaved. Who knows how God might use us for His church throughout the whole world! Is it not worthwhile to sacrifice everything and to beseech God without ceasing to give us full victory over the prayerlessness that has brought us shame?

Why do I write these things and extol so highly the blessedness of victory over "the sin that so easily besets us," and which has so robbed us of the power that God intended for us? Let me answer this. I know all too well what weak concepts we have concerning the promises and the power of God. I see how prone we are to backsliding, to limiting God's power, and to deeming it impossible for Him to do greater things than we have seen. It is a glorious thing to get to know God in a new way in our prayer time. That, however, is only the beginning. It is something still greater and more glorious to know God as the All-Sufficient One and to wait on His Spirit to open our hearts and minds to receive the great things, the new things that He longs to bestow on those who wait for Him.

God's purpose is to encourage faith in His children, His servants, so that they understand and rely upon the unspeakable greatness and omnipotence of God, so that they take literally, in a childlike spirit, this word: "Now to him who is able to do immeasurably more than all we ask or imagine, according to his power that is at work within us, to him be glory in the church and in Christ Jesus throughout all generations, for ever and ever! Amen" (Ephesians 3:20–21). Oh, that we knew what a great and glorious God we have!

You may ask: "May not this note of certain victory become a snare and lead to levity and pride?" Undoubtedly. That which is the highest and best on earth is always liable to abuse. How then can we be saved from this? Through nothing more than true prayer, which brings us into contact with God. The holiness of God, sought for in persistent prayer, will cover our sinfulness. The omnipotence and greatness of God will cause us to acknowledge our unworthiness. Fellowship with God in Jesus Christ will lead us to realize that there is in us no good thing, and that we can have fellowship with God only as our faith causes us to humble ourselves as Christ humbled himself.

Prayer is not merely coming to God to ask something of Him. It is, above all, fellowship with God and being brought under the power of His holiness and love, until He takes possession of us and stamps our entire nature with the lowliness of Christ, which is the secret of all true worship.

In Christ Jesus we draw near to the Father just as those who have died with Christ and have entirely given up their own life, like those in whom He lives and who He enables to say: "Christ lives in me." What we have said about the work that the Lord Jesus does in us to deliver us from prayerlessness is true not only of the beginning of the life of prayer and of the joy that a new experience of power to pray causes us but also for the whole life of prayer day by day. Through Him we have access to the Father. In this, as in the whole spiritual life, Christ is all. They saw no man but Jesus.

May God strengthen us to believe that there is certain victory prepared for us and that the blessing will be more than the heart of man has conceived! God will do this for those who love Him.

This does not come to us all at once. God has great patience with His children. He bears with us in fatherly patience at our slow progress. Let each child of God rejoice in all that God's Word promises. The stronger our faith, the more earnestly will we persevere to the end.

Chapter 7

The More Abundant Life

Our Lord spoke this word concerning the more abundant life when He said that He had come to give His life for His sheep: "I have come that they may have life, and have it to the full" (John 10:10). A man may have life, and still through lack of nourishment or through illness there may be no abundance of life or power. This was the distinction between the Old Testament and the New. In the former there was life under the law but not the abundance of grace of the New Testament. Christ had given life to His disciples, but they could receive the abundant life only through His resurrection and the gift of the Holy Spirit.

All true Christians have received life from Christ. The majority, however, know nothing about the more abundant life that He is willing to bestow. Paul speaks constantly of this. He says about himself that the grace of God was exceedingly abundant: "I can do all things through Christ who strengthens me. Thanks be to God, who always causes us to triumph in Christ. We are more than conquerors through him that loved us."

We have spoken of the sin of prayerlessness, the means of deliverance, and how to be kept free from it. What has been said on these points is all included in that expression of

Christ: "I have come that they may have life, and have it to the full" (John 10:10). It is of utmost importance for us to understand this more abundant life, because for a true life of prayer it is necessary that we walk in an ever-increasing experience of that overflowing life.

It is possible for us to begin this conflict against prayerlessness in dependence on Christ, looking to Him to be assisted and kept in it, and still be disappointed. This is the time when prayerlessness must be looked upon as the one sin against which we must strive. It must be recognized as part of the whole life of the flesh and as being closely connected with other sins that spring from the same source. We forget that the flesh and all its affections, whether manifested in the body or the soul, must be regarded as crucified and be handed over to death. We must not be satisfied with a weakened life, but must seek an abundant life. We must surrender ourselves entirely so that the Spirit may take full possession of us and manifest His life in us so that our spiritual being will be completely transformed.

What is it that particularly constitutes this abundant life? We cannot too often repeat it or in different ways too often explain it: the abundant life is nothing less than Jesus having full mastery over our entire being through the power of the Holy Spirit. As the Spirit makes known in us the fullness of Christ and the abundant life that He gives, it will be done chiefly in three aspects:

1. *As the Crucified One.* Not merely as the One who died for us to atone for our sins, but as He who has taken us up with himself on the cross to die with Him, and who now works out in us the power of His cross and death. You have true fellowship with Christ when you can say: "I have been crucified with Christ. He, the Crucified One, lives in me."

The feelings, the disposition that was in Him, His lowliness and obedience even to death on the cross—these were what He referred to when He said of the Holy Spirit: "He shall take of mine, and shall show it unto you"—not as an instruction, but as childlike participation of the same life that was in Him.

Do you desire the Holy Spirit to take full possession of you so as to cause the crucified Christ to dwell in you? This is exactly the purpose for which He has been given, and this He will surely accomplish in all who yield themselves to Him.

2. *As the Risen One.* The Scripture frequently mentions the resurrection in connection with the wonder-working power of God by which Christ was raised from the dead and from which comes the assurance of "his incomparably great power toward us who believe. That power is like the working of his mighty strength, which he exerted in Christ when he raised him from the dead" (Ephesians 1:19–20). Do not pass over these words too quickly. Read them again. No matter how powerless and weak you feel, recognize the truth that the omnipotence of God is working in you; and if you believe, will give you daily a share in the resurrection of His Son.

Yes, the Holy Spirit can fill you with the joy and victory of the resurrection of Christ as the power of your daily life right in the midst of the trials and temptations of this world. Let the cross humble you to the death of self. God will work out the heavenly life in you through His Spirit. How little we have understood that it is entirely the work of the Holy Spirit to make us partakers of the crucified and risen Christ and to conform us to His life and death!

3. *As the Glorified One.* The glorified Christ is He who

baptizes with the Holy Spirit. When the Lord Jesus himself was baptized with the Spirit, it was because He had humbled himself and offered himself to take part in John's baptism of repentance—a baptism for sinners—in the Jordan River. Even so, when He took upon himself the work of redemption, He received the Holy Spirit to fit Him for His work from that hour until on the cross "He offered himself without spot to God." Do you want this glorified Christ to baptize you with the Holy Spirit? Then offer yourself to Him for His service to further His great work of making known to sinners the love of the Father.

God help us to understand what a great thing it is to receive the Holy Spirit with power from the glorified Jesus! It means a willingness—a longing of the soul—to work for Him and if need be to suffer for Him. You have known and loved your Lord, you have worked for Him and have had blessing in that work, but the Lord has more than that to bestow. By the power of the Holy Spirit, He can so work in us, in our brothers and sisters around us, and in the ministers of the church so as to fill our hearts with adoring wonder and praise.

Have you grasped this truth? The abundant life is neither more nor less than the full life of Christ as the Crucified One, the Risen One, and the Glorified One, who baptizes with the Holy Spirit and reveals himself in our hearts and lives as Lord of all within us.

Not long ago I read an interesting thought: "Live in what must be." Do not live limited by your human imagination of what is possible. Live in the Word—in the love and infinite faithfulness of the Lord Jesus. Even though it goes slowly, with many a faltering step, the faith that always thanks

Him—not for experiences but for the promises on which it can rely—goes on from strength to strength, ever increasing in the blessed assurance that God himself will perfect His work in us.

Chapter 8

The Example of
Our Lord

The connection between the prayer life and the Spirit life is close and indissoluble. Not only do we receive the Spirit through prayer, but also a continuous prayer life is indispensable to the Spirit life. Only as I give myself continually to prayer can I expect to be led continually by the Spirit.

This was very evident in the life of our Lord. A study of His life will give us a picture of the power of prayer.

Consider His baptism. When He was baptized and prayed, heaven was opened, and the Holy Spirit came down upon Him. Christ's surrender of himself to the sinner's baptism in the Jordan was also a surrender of himself to the sinner's death. God desired to crown that surrender with the gift of His Spirit for the work that He would accomplish. But this could not have taken place had He not prayed. In the fellowship of worship the Spirit was bestowed upon Him to lead Him out into the desert to spend forty days in prayer and fasting. Mark 1:32–35 says, "That evening after sunset the people brought to Jesus all the sick and demon-possessed. The whole town gathered at the door. Very early in the morning, while it was still dark, Jesus got up, left the house and went off to a solitary place, where he prayed."

The work of the day and evening had exhausted Him. In His healing of the sick and casting out devils, power had gone out of Him. While others slept, He went away to pray and to renew His strength in communion with His Father. He needed this time with God—otherwise He would not have been ready for the new day. The holy work of delivering souls demands constant renewal through fellowship with God.

Think of the calling of the apostles as recorded in Luke 6:12–13: "One of those days Jesus went out to a mountain-side to pray, and spent the night praying to God. When morning came, he called his disciples to him and chose twelve of them, whom he also designated apostles." It is clear that if anyone wants to do God's work, he must take time for fellowship with Him to receive His wisdom and power. The dependence and helplessness we all experience opens the way to give God an opportunity to reveal His power. Choosing the apostles who would follow Christ's example was of great importance for the work of the early church. It had God's blessing and seal, and the stamp of prayer was on it.

Read Luke 9:18, 20: "Once when Jesus was praying in private and his disciples were with him, he asked them, 'Who do the crowds say I am?' Peter answered, 'The Christ of God.' The Lord had prayed that the Father might reveal to them who He was. It was in answer to that prayer that Peter said, 'The Christ of God'; and the Lord then said: 'This was not revealed to you by man, but by my Father in heaven' " (Matthew 16:17). This great confession was the fruit of prayer.

Read on in Luke 9:28–36: "He took Peter, John and James with him and went up onto a mountain to pray. As he was praying, the appearance of his face changed. . . . A voice came from the cloud, saying, 'This is my Son, whom I have chosen; listen to him.' " Christ desired that for the strengthening of their faith God might give them assurance from heaven that He was the Son of God. Jesus' prayer that who He was might be revealed to His disciples was answered on the Mount of Transfiguration.

Does it not become even more clear that what God wills to accomplish on earth needs prayer as its indispensable condition? There was only one way for Christ and so for believers: a heart and mouth open toward heaven in believing prayer will certainly not be put to shame.

Read Luke 11:1–13: "One day Jesus was praying in a certain place. When he finished, one of his disciples said to him, 'Lord, teach us to pray.' " And then He gave them that inexhaustible prayer: "Our Father, who art in heaven . . ." In this He showed what was going on in His heart when He prayed that God's name might be hallowed, His kingdom come, His will be done, and all of this "on earth as it is in heaven." How will this ever come to pass? It will come about through prayer. The Lord's Prayer has been uttered through the ages by countless millions to their unspeakable comfort. But do not forget: it was born out of the prayer of our Lord Jesus. He had been praying himself and therefore was able to give the answer in the form of a prayer.

John 14:16 says, "I will ask the Father, and he will give you another Counselor." The entire dispensation of the New Testament, with the wonderful outpouring of the Holy Spirit, is the outcome of the prayer of the Lord Jesus. It is as though God had impressed on the gift of the Holy Spirit this seal: in answer to the prayer of the Lord Jesus, and later of His disciples, the Holy Spirit will surely come. But it will be in answer to prayer like that of our Lord, in which He took time to be alone with God, and in that prayer offered himself wholly to God.

Read John 17, the high-priestly, most holy prayer! Here the Son prays first for himself that the Father will glorify Him by giving Him power for the cross, by raising Him from the dead, and by setting Him at His right hand. These great things could not take place except through prayer. Prayer had the power to obtain them.

Afterward He prayed for His disciples that the Father might preserve them from the Evil One, keep them from the world, and sanctify them. Further on He prayed for all those who through the Word might believe on Him, that all might be one in love even as the Father and the Son are one. This prayer gives us a glimpse into the remarkable relationship between the Father and the Son. It teaches us that all the blessings of heaven come and continue to come through the prayer of Him who is at God's right hand and prays for us. But it teaches us also that all these blessings must in the same manner be desired and asked for by us. The whole nature and glory of God's blessings consist in this: they must be obtained in answer to prayer by hearts entirely surrendered to Him and by hearts that believe in the power of prayer.

Now we look at the most stunning instance of all: in Gethsemane, according to His habit, our Lord consulted and arranged with the Father the work He had to do on earth. First, He besought Him in agony and blood to allow the cup to pass from Him. When He understood that this could not be, He prayed for strength to drink the cup and surrendered himself with the words: "Your will be done." He was able to meet the Enemy full of courage, and in the power of God gave himself over to death on the cross. *He prayed.*

Why have God's children so little faith in the glory of prayer as the great power for subjecting our own wills to that of God as well as for the confident carrying out of the work of God in spite of our great weakness? Learn from our Lord Jesus how impossible it is to walk with God, obtain God's blessing or leading, or do His work joyously and fruitfully apart from close, unbroken fellowship with the One who is our living fountain of spiritual life and power.

Think over this simple study of the prayer life of our Lord Jesus. Then with prayer for the leading of the Holy Spirit, endeavor to learn from God's Word about the life that the Lord Jesus Christ bestows upon every Christian and then supports. It is nothing other than the life of daily prayer. Let every minister of the gospel recognize how entirely useless it is to attempt to do the work of the Lord in any other way than the way He did it. Let us as layworkers believe that we are set free from the ordinary business of the world, that we may above everything have time, in our Savior's name and by His Spirit and in oneness with Him, to ask for and obtain blessing for the world.

Chapter 9

The Holy Spirit and Prayer

Is it not unfortunate that our thoughts about the Holy Spirit are so often coupled with grief and self-reproach? Yet He bears the name of Comforter [Counselor, in the NIV] and is given to lead us to find in Christ our highest delight and joy. Sadder still is the fact that He who dwells within us to comfort us is often grieved by us because we will not permit Him to accomplish His work of love. All this prayerlessness in the church must be a source of inexpressible pain to the Holy Spirit. Surely the low energy and utter helplessness so often found in us is because we do not permit the Holy Spirit to lead us.

God grant that our meditation on the work of the Holy Spirit may cause rejoicing and the strengthening of our faith!

The Holy Spirit is the Spirit of prayer. He is called in Zechariah 12:10 "a spirit of grace and supplication." Twice in Paul's epistles there is a remarkable reference to Him in the matter of prayer: "For you did not receive a spirit that makes you a slave again to fear, but you received the Spirit of sonship. And by him we cry, '*Abba*, Father'" (Romans 8:15, emphasis added). "Because you are sons, God sent the Spirit of his Son into our hearts, the Spirit who calls out, 'Abba, Father'" (Galatians 4:6, emphasis added). Have you ever meditated on the words *Abba, Father*? In that name our Savior offered His greatest prayer to the Father, accompanied by the total surrender and sacrifice of His life and love. The Holy Spirit is given for the express purpose of teaching us right from the very beginning of our Christian life to utter that word in childlike trust and surrender. In one of these passages we read, "We cry", in the other, "the Spirit calls." What a wonderful blending of the divine and the human cooperation in prayer. What proof that God has done His utmost to make prayer as natural and effectual as the cry of a child to an earthly father when he says, "Abba, Father."

And is it not proof that the Holy Spirit is often a stranger in the church when prayer for which God has made such provision is regarded as a task and a burden? Does not this teach us to look for the deep root of prayerlessness in our ignorance of and disobedience to the divine Instructor whom the Father has commissioned to teach us to pray?

If we wish to understand this truth even more clearly, we can look at Romans 8:26–27: "In the same way, the Spirit helps us in our weakness. We do not know what we ought to pray for, but the Spirit himself intercedes for us with groans that words cannot express. And he who searches our hearts knows the mind of the Spirit, because the Spirit intercedes for the saints in accordance with God's will." Is it not clear? The Christian left to himself does not know how to pray or what he ought to pray for. But God has stooped to meet us in this helplessness of ours by giving us the Holy Spirit to pray for us. That operation of His Spirit is deeper than our thoughts or feelings, but is acknowledged and answered by God.

Our first work, therefore, ought to be to come into God's presence not with our ignorant prayers, not with many words and thoughts, but in the confidence that the divine work of the Holy Spirit is being carried out within us. This confidence will encourage reverence and quietness and will also enable us, in dependence on the help that the Spirit gives, to lay our desires and deepest needs before God. The supreme lesson for every prayer is first of all to commit to the leading of the Holy Spirit and in total dependence on Him to give Him first place. Through Him your prayer will have value you cannot imagine. Through Him also you will learn to express your desires in the name of Christ.

Such faith would be protection against listlessness and despair in our place of prayer! Think of it! In every prayer the triune God takes a part—the Father who hears, the Son in whose name we pray, and the Spirit who prays for us and in us. How important it is that we are in right relationship to the Holy Spirit and that we understand His work!

The following points demand serious consideration.

1. *Let us firmly believe that the Spirit of God's Son, the Holy Spirit, is in us.* Do not assume that you know this and have no need to reconsider it. It is a thought so important and so divine that it can gain entrance to our hearts and be retained there only by the Holy Spirit. "The Spirit bears witness with our spirit." Our position ought to be that of reckoning with full assurance of faith that our heart is His temple and that He dwells within us and rules the soul and the body. Let us thank God heartily whenever we pray that we have His Spirit in us to teach us to pray. Thanksgiving will draw our hearts toward God and keep us in fellowship with Him;

it will take our attention from ourselves and give the Spirit room in our hearts.

No wonder we have been lacking in prayer and have felt this work too hard for us: we have tried to have fellowship with the eternal God apart from His Spirit, who reveals the Father and the Son to us.

2. *As we put this faith into practice with the certainty that the Spirit dwells and works in us, there must also be an understanding of all that He desires to accomplish in us.* His work in prayer is closely connected with His other work. In an earlier chapter we saw that His first and greatest work is to reveal Christ in His omnipresent love and power. So in prayer the Holy Spirit will constantly remind us of Christ, of His blood and His name, as the sure basis of our being heard.

Then, as the Spirit of holiness, He will teach us to recognize, hate, and be done with sin. He is the Spirit of light and wisdom, who leads us into the heavenly secret of God's overflowing grace. He is the Spirit of love and power, who teaches us to witness for Christ and to labor for souls with tender pity. The more closely I associate all these blessings with the Spirit, the more I will be convinced of His deity and the more ready I will be to commit myself to His guidance as I give myself to prayer. What a different life mine would be if I knew the Spirit as the Spirit of prayer! Another thing I need constantly to learn is:

3. *The Spirit desires full possession of my life.* We pray for more of the Spirit, and we pray well if alongside this prayer we hold the truth that the Spirit wants more of us. The Spirit would possess us entirely. Just as my soul has my whole body for its dwelling place and service, so the Holy Spirit would have my body and soul as His dwelling place, entirely under

His control. No one can continue long and earnestly in prayer without perceiving that the Spirit is gently leading him to an entirely new consecration of which he previously knew nothing. "I seek you with my whole heart." The Spirit will make such words more and more the motto of our lives. He will cause us to recognize that what remains in us of double-mindedness is truly sinful. He will reveal Christ as the almighty deliverer from all sin, who is always near to defend us. He will lead us in this way in prayer. He will help us to forget ourselves. He will make us willing to offer ourselves for training as intercessors to whom God can entrust the fulfillment of His plans and who day and night cry to Him to avenge His church of her adversary.

God, help us to know the Spirit and to revere Him as the Spirit of prayer!

— Chapter 10 —

A Proper Knowledge of What Sin Is

To understand grace and to understand Christ aright, we must understand what sin is. How can we come to this understanding? Through the light of God and His Word.

Come with me to the beginning of the Bible. We see man created by God after His image and pronounced by his Creator to be very good. Then sin entered. It was rebellion against God. Adam and Eve were driven out of the Garden and brought, along with untold millions, under the curse and utter ruin. *That was the work of sin.*

Let us look further into Scripture at the story of Noah and his ark on Mount Ararat. Godlessness had become so rampant among men that God saw no remedy but to destroy humankind from the face of the earth. *That was the work of sin.*

What about Sinai? God wanted to establish His covenant with a new nation: the people of Israel. But because of man's sinfulness, He could do this only by appearing in darkness and lightning so frightening that even Moses was afraid and trembled. And before the end of the giving of the law, the message came that anyone who did not continue in all things written in the book of the law was cursed. *It was sin that made that decree necessary.*

When we visit Mount Calvary, we get a taste of what sin is: we see the hatred and enmity with which the world cast out and crucified the Son of God. Here sin reached its climax. Christ was made sin and became a curse as the only way to destroy the power of sin. In the agony of Gethsemane, when He prayed that He might be spared the terrible cup, and in excruciating pain on the cross with its deep darkness and desertion by the Father, He cried out, "My God, my God, why have you forsaken me?" we get a faint glimpse of the curse and the indescribable suffering sin brings. If anything can cause us to hate and detest sin, it is seeing Christ on that bitter cross.

Finally, let us look at the judgment seat of God on the Last Day and the bottomless pit of darkness, where countless souls will plunge under the sentence of Matthew 25:41: "Depart from me, you who are cursed, into the eternal fire prepared for the devil and his angels." When these words truly penetrate our hearts, they will fill us with a not-to-be-forgotten horror of sin.

Remember that you are a child of God. Sometimes you commit sin: you allow it to fulfill its desires. Are you forced to cry out with shame: "Woe unto me because of my sin"? The great power of sin is that it blinds us so that we do not recognize its true character. Even the Christian finds an excuse, thinking that he can never be perfect, and that daily sin is a necessity. He is so accustomed to the idea of sinning that he has lost the ability to grieve over it. But there can be no real progress in grace apart from an increased consciousness of the sin and guilt of every transgression against God.

And there cannot be a more important question than this: "How can I regain the lost tenderness of conscience and become prepared to offer to God the sacrifice of a broken heart?"

Scripture teaches us the way. Remember what God thinks about sin: His holiness burns against it; He sacrificed His Son to conquer sin and to deliver us from it. Wait in God's presence until His holiness shines upon you, and you cry out with Isaiah: "Woe unto me, for I am undone!"

Remember the cross and what the love of Christ endured there; what unspeakable pain sin caused Him. Take time, so that the suffering of Christ on the cross may have its full effect and influence. Think of sin as nothing less than giving your hand over to Satan and his power. This is one of the awful results of our prayerlessness and of our quick, careless "waiting" before God: a true knowledge of sin is all but lost.

Think not only of what redemption cost Christ but also of the fact that Christ is offered by the Holy Spirit as a gift of grace through whom divine forgiveness and renewal come to us. Ask how such love should be repaid. If only time were taken to linger in God's presence and ask such questions, the Spirit of God would accomplish His work of conviction of sin. He would teach us to take an entirely new viewpoint of sin. The thought would begin to arise in our hearts that we have truly been redeemed, so that in Christ's power we may live every day as partners in the great victory He obtained over sin on the cross and begin to manifest it in our walk.

Are you beginning to see that the sin of prayerlessness has had a greater effect than you first thought? Because of hasty and superficial communion with God, the sense of sin becomes weak and there is no motive strong enough to help you to hate sin and flee from it. Nothing except secret, humble, constant fellowship with God can teach you as His child to hate sin as God hates it. Nothing but the close fellowship and unceasing power of the living Christ can make it possible for you to understand what sin is and to detest it. Without this deeper understanding of sin, we cannot truly appropriate the victory that Christ made possible for us.

Chapter 11

The Holiness of God

It has often been said that the church has lost the concept of sin and the holiness of God. In the secret place of prayer we may learn anew how to give God's holiness the place it should have in our faith and our life. If you do not know how to spend half an hour in prayer, take up the subject of God's holiness. Bow before Him and give God time so that you may know His presence, and He may speak to you. It is an effort at first, but one that results in great blessing.

To strengthen yourself in the practice of His holy presence, take up the Word. Read the book of Leviticus and notice how God five times gives the command: "Consecrate yourselves and be holy, because I am holy" (11:44–45; 19:2; 20:7, 26). Still more frequent is the expression: "I am the Lord that sanctifies you." This great thought is carried over into the New Testament. Peter says (1 Peter 1:15–16): "But just as he who called you is holy, so be holy in all you do; for it is written: 'Be holy, because I am holy.'" Paul writes in his first epistle (1 Thessalonians 3:13; 4:7; 5:24): "May he strengthen your hearts so that you will be blameless and holy in the presence of our God and Father when our Lord Jesus comes with all his holy ones. For God did not call us to be impure, but to live a holy life. The one who calls you is faithful and he will do it."

Nothing but the knowledge of God as the Holy One will make us holy. How are we to obtain that knowledge of God unless we go alone to Him in the place of prayer? It is utterly impossible unless we take time and allow the holiness of God to reveal itself to us. How can anyone on earth obtain intimate knowledge of another if he does not associate with that person and remain under that one's influence? And how can God himself sanctify us if we do not take time to be brought under the power of the glory of His holiness? Nowhere can we get to know the holiness of God and come under its influence and power except in private prayer. It has been well said: "No man can expect to make progress in holiness who is not often and long alone with God."

And what is the holiness of God? It is the highest, most glorious, most all-embracing of all the attributes of God. *Holiness* is the most profound word in the Bible. It is a word that is at home in heaven. Both the Old and New Testaments tell us this. Isaiah heard the seraphs with veiled faces cry out: "Holy, holy, holy is the Lord Almighty; the whole earth is full of his glory" (6:3). John heard the four living creatures say, "Holy, holy, holy is the Lord God Almighty, who was, and is, and is to come" (Revelation 4:8). This is the highest expression of God's glory in heaven by beings who live in His immediate presence and bow low before Him. Do we dare imagine that we—by thinking, reading, and hearing—can understand or become partakers of the holiness of God? We need to begin to thank God that we have our private place of prayer, a place where we can be alone with Him.

If we remain prayerless, let our hearts be deeply ashamed. By so doing we make it impossible for God to impart His

holiness to us. Let us ask God to forgive us this sin and to draw us to himself by His heavenly grace and to strengthen us to have fellowship with Him, the One who is holy.

The meaning of the words *the holiness of God* is not easily expressed. But we may begin by saying that they imply the unspeakable aversion and hatred with which God regards sin. If you want to understand what that means, remember that He preferred to see His Son die than that sin should reign in us. Think of the Son of God, who gave up His life rather than act in the smallest matter against the will of the Father. He had such a hatred of sin that He preferred to die rather than let men be held in its power. That is something of the holiness of God; it is a pledge that He will do everything for us in order to deliver us from sin. Holiness is the fire of God that will consume sin in us and make us holy sacrifices, pure and acceptable before Him. For this reason the Spirit came down as fire. He is the Spirit of God's holiness, the Spirit of sanctification in us.

Think about the holiness of God and bow in lowliness before Him until your heart is filled with the assurance of what He will do for you. Take a week, if necessary, to read and reread the words of God on this great truth until your heart is brought under the conviction: "This is the glory of the secret place of prayer, to be able to converse with God, the Holy One, and to bow in deep humility and shame before Him, because we have so offended Him and His love through our prayerlessness." There we shall receive the assurance that He will again take us into fellowship with himself. No one can expect to understand and receive the holiness of God who is not often and long alone with Him.

Someone has said that the holiness of God is the expression of the unspeakable distance by which He in His

righteousness are separated from us, and yet also of the unspeakable nearness in which He in His love longs to hold fellowship with us and dwell in us. Bow in humble reverence as you think of the immeasurable distance between you and God. Bow in childlike confidence in the strong desire of His heart to be united with you in the deepest intimacy, and reckon most confidently on Him to reveal something of His holiness to the soul that thirsts after Him and waits upon Him and is quiet before Him.

Notice how the two sides of the holiness of God are united in the cross. So terrible was the aversion and anger of God against our sin that Christ was left in darkness; God had to hide His face from Christ when sin was laid upon Him. Still, so deep was the love of God toward us, and He so desired to be united to us, that He spared not His Son but gave Him over to unutterable sufferings so that He might receive us in union with Christ into His holiness and embrace us as His beloved children. It was of this suffering that our Lord Jesus said, "For them I sanctify myself, that they too may be truly sanctified" (John 17:19). He is our sanctification, and we are holy in Him.

I ask that you not think lightly of that grace: you have a holy God who longs to make you holy. Obey the voice of God that calls you to give time to Him in the stillness of your prayer room so that He may cause His holiness to rest on you. Let it be your habit every day, in the secrecy of your place of prayer, to meet the holy God. You will be repaid for the inconvenience it may cost you. The reward will be sure and rich. You will learn to hate sin and to regard it as cursed but conquered. The new nature will give you an abhorrence of sin. The living Jesus, the holy God, will as Conqueror be your strength, and you will begin to believe the great prom-

ise contained in 1 Thessalonians 5:23–24: "May God himself, the God of peace, sanctify you through and through. May your whole spirit, soul and body be kept blameless at the coming of our Lord Jesus Christ. The one who calls you is faithful and he will do it."

Chapter 12

The Importance of Obedience

In opposition to sin stands obedience. "For just as through the disobedience of the one man the many were made sinners, so also through the obedience of the one man the many will be made righteous. You have been set free from sin and have become slaves to righteousness" (Romans 5:19; 6:18). In connection with all that has been said about sin and the new life and the reception of the Holy Spirit, we must always give to obedience the place assigned to it by God.

It was because Christ humbled himself and became obedient unto death, even death on the cross, that God so highly exalted Him. In this connection Paul exhorts us: "Your attitude should be the same as that of Christ Jesus" (Philippians 2:5). We see, above everything else, that the obedience of Christ, so pleasing to God, must become the basic characteristic of our disposition and of our entire walk. Just as a servant knows that he must first obey his master in all things, so the surrender to an implicit and unquestioning obedience to God must become the essential characteristic of our lives.

How little this is understood by Christians! How many

allow themselves to be misled and rest satisfied with the belief that sin is a necessity and that one must sin every day! It would be difficult to say how much harm is done by this mistake. It is one of the main reasons why the sin of disobedience is so seldom recognized. I have heard Christians laughingly speak about the cause of darkness and weakness in their lives as "just disobedience again." Don't we as quickly as possible try to get rid of an employee who is habitually insubordinate? But when a child of God is disobedient every day, we do not regard it as anything extraordinary. Disobedience may be daily acknowledged, but there is no turning away from it.

Perhaps this is why so much prayer is made for the power of the Holy Spirit and yet so few answers come. We read, "God has given His Holy Spirit to them that obey Him." Every child of God has received the Holy Spirit when he was born again. If he uses the measure of the Holy Spirit that he has with the definite purpose of being obedient to the utmost, then God can and will favor him with further manifestations of the Spirit's power. But if he permits disobedience to get the upper hand day after day, he need not be surprised if his prayer for more of the Spirit remains unanswered.

We have already said that the Spirit desires to possess more of us. How can we fully surrender ourselves to Him other than by being obedient? The Scripture says that we are to be led by the Spirit and that we must walk by the Spirit. My right relationship to the Holy Spirit is that I allow myself to be guided and ruled by Him. Obedience is the most important factor in our whole relationship to God.

Notice how the Lord Jesus, giving His great promise about the Holy Spirit on His last night, emphasized this point: "If you love me, you will obey what I command. And I will ask the Father, and he will give you another Counselor to be with you forever" (John 14:15–16). Obedience was essential as preparation for the reception of the Spirit. He often repeated this thought: "Whoever has my commands and obeys them, he is the one who loves me. He who loves me will be loved by my Father, and I too will love him and show myself to him" (John 14:21). So also in verse 23: "If anyone loves me, he will obey my teaching. My Father will love him, and we will come to him and make our home with him." And in chapter 15 of John, verse 7: "If you remain in me and my words remain in you, ask whatever you wish, and it will be given you." And verses 10 and 14: "If you obey my commands, you will remain in my love, just as I have obeyed my Father's commands and remain in his love. You are my friends if you do what I command."

Can words more plainly declare that our life in this new dispensation since the resurrection of Christ depends on obedience? That was the attitude of Christ's life. He lived to do not His own will but the will of the Father. And He cannot with His Spirit make an abiding home in the heart of one who does not surrender completely to a life of obedience.

It is truly sad how few are concerned about this disobedience! How little we believe that Christ asks for, expects this, from us—because He has undertaken to make it possible for us. How much is it manifested in our prayer, our walk, or in the depths of our spiritual life that we seek to please the Lord in all things? Too seldom we mention our disobedience or say, "I will be sorry for my sin."

But is obedience really possible? It certainly is for the

man who believes that Christ Jesus is his sanctification and relies on Him.

It is impossible for a man whose eyes have not yet been opened to see that Christ can at once forgive his sin. Such a man also finds it impossible to see that there is in Christ a sure promise of power to accomplish all that God desires of His child. Just as we found the fullness of forgiveness through faith, so through a new act of faith deliverance from the dominion of sin that so easily ensnares us is obtained. And by faith the abiding blessing of this continuous experience of Christ's keeping power becomes ours. This faith obtains new insight into promises whose meaning was not previously understood: "May the God of peace, who through the blood of the eternal covenant brought back from the dead our Lord Jesus, that great Shepherd of the sheep, equip you with everything good for doing his will, and may he work in us what is pleasing to him, through Jesus Christ" (Hebrews 13:20–21). "To him who is able to keep you from falling and to present you before his glorious presence without fault and with great joy—to the only God our Savior be glory, majesty, power and authority, through Jesus Christ our Lord" (Jude 24–25). "Therefore, my brothers, be all the more eager to make your calling and election sure. For if you do these things, you will never fall" (2 Peter 1:10). "May he strengthen your hearts so that you will be blameless and holy in the presence of our God and Father when our Lord Jesus comes with all his holy ones" (1 Thessalonians 3:13). "But the Lord is faithful, and he will strengthen and protect you from the evil one" (2 Thessalonians 3:3).

The fulfillment of these and other promises is secured for us in Christ. Just as certainly as the forgiveness of sin is assured to us in Him, so also is power against new or fresh attacks of sin assured to us. Then for the first time we understand that faith can confidently rely fully upon Christ and His abiding protection.

This faith sheds a totally new light on the life of obedience. *Christ holds himself responsible to work this out in me every moment, if I only trust Him for it.* I begin to understand the important phrase with which Paul begins and closes the book of Romans: "obedience that comes from faith" (Romans 1:5; 16:26). Faith brings me to the Lord Jesus not only for forgiveness of sin but also every moment to enjoy the power that enables me as a child of God to abide in Him and to be numbered among His obedient children. It is written of these children that as He who has called them is holy, so they also may be holy in all their behavior. Everything depends on whether or not I believe on the whole Christ with the fullness of His grace, and that He will be—not now and then but every moment—the strength of my life. Such faith will lead to an obedience that will enable me to "walk worthy of the Lord unto all pleasing, being fruitful in every good work, strengthened with all might, according to his glorious power."

The soul that feeds on such promises will experience instead of the disobedience of self-effort all that the obedience of faith means. All such promises have their measure, their certainty, and their strength in the living Christ.

Chapter 13

The Victorious Life

We viewed chapter 7, "The More Abundant Life," mainly from the side of our Lord Jesus. We saw that there is to be found in him—the Crucified One, the Risen One, and the Glorified One, who baptizes with the Holy Spirit—all that is needed for a life of abundant grace. Now, in speaking of "The Victorious Life," we will look from another standpoint. We want to see how a Christian can live as a true victor. We have often said that the prayer life is not something that can be improved upon in and of itself. So intimately is it bound up with the entire spiritual life that only when that whole life (previously marked by a lack of prayer) becomes renewed and sanctified can prayer have its rightful place of power. We must not be satisfied with less than the victorious life to which God calls His children.

Our Lord in the seven letters to the churches in Revelation concludes with a promise to each for those who overcome. The phrase "he that overcomes" is repeated seven times; and with it some glorious promises are given. They were given even to churches like Ephesus that had "forsaken its first love," to Sardis, that "[had] a reputation of being alive, but was dead," and Laodicea with her lukewarmness and self-satisfaction—as proof that if they would only repent, they might win the crown of victory. The call comes to every Christian to strive for the crown. If everything is not sacrificed to gain the victory, how is it possible to be a healthy Christian or to preach in the power of the Spirit? It is not; it is impossible.

How do we attain victory, then? The answer is simple. All is in Christ. "Thanks be to God, who always leads us in triumphal procession in Christ" (2 Corinthians 2:14). "In all these things we are more than conquerors through him who loved us" (Romans 8:37). It all depends on our right relationship to Christ, our complete surrender, perfect faith, and unbroken fellowship with Him. But how do you attain to all of this? These simple guidelines show the way by which the full enjoyment of what is prepared for you in Christ may be yours: (1) a new discovery of sin; (2) a new surrender to Christ; (3) a new faith in the power that will make it possible for you to persevere.

1. *A new discovery of sin.* In Romans 3 we find described the knowledge of sin that is necessary for repentance and forgiveness: "Now we know that whatever the law says, it says to those who are under the law, so that every mouth may be silenced and the whole world held accountable to God" (v. 19). And so you recognized your sin more or less consciously, confessed it, and obtained mercy. But if you would lead a victorious life, something more is needed. This begins with the recognition that in you, that is, in your flesh, there dwells no good thing (Romans 7:18). In the inner man you delight in the law of God, but you see another law in your members bringing you into captivity to the law of sin, and compelling you to cry out: "What a wretched man I am! Who will rescue me from this body of death?" (vv. 23–24). This is not like your experience at conversion, when you

thought over your few or many sins. This work goes much deeper. You find that as a Christian you have no power to do the good that you want to do. You must be brought to a new and deeper insight into the sin of your nature, and even though you are a Christian, you must see your utter weakness to live as you ought. You will learn to cry out: "What a wretched man I am! Who will rescue me from this body of death?"

The answer to this question is "Thanks be to God— through Jesus Christ our Lord!" (v. 25). Then follows the revelation of what there is in Christ. It is not limited to what is given in Romans 3. It is more. I am in Christ Jesus, and the law of the Spirit of life in Christ has made me free from the law of sin and death under which I was bound. I have been made free by the law (or power) of the life of the Spirit in Christ, and now am called in a new sense and by a new surrender to acknowledge Christ as the giver of the victory.

2. *A new surrender to Christ.* You may have used these words *surrender* and *consecration* many times but without a right understanding of what they mean. As you have been brought by the teaching of Romans 7 to a complete sense of the hopelessness of leading a true Christian life or a true prayer life by your own efforts, you begin to realize that the Lord Jesus must take you up by His own power in an entirely new way, and must take possession of you by His Spirit to an entirely new degree. This alone can preserve you from constantly sinning. Only this can make you truly victorious. This leads you to look away from yourself, to get free from yourself, and to expect everything to come from the Lord Jesus.

If we begin to understand this, we are prepared to admit that in our nature there is nothing good; it is under a curse and is nailed with Christ to His cross. We come to see what Paul means when he says that we are dead to sin by the death of Christ. Thus we obtain a share of the glorious resurrection life that is in Him. With this insight we are encouraged to believe that Christ through His life in us, through His continual indwelling, can keep us. Just as we had no rest until we knew He had received us at our conversion, so now we feel the need of coming to Him to receive from Him the assurance that He has undertaken to keep us by the power of His resurrection life. And so we feel that there must be an act as definite as His reception of us at conversion by which He gives us the assurance of victory. And although it appears to us to be too great and too much, still the man who casts himself without plea into the arms of Christ will experience that He does indeed receive us into such a fellowship as will make us, right from the beginning, "more than conquerors."

3. *A new faith in the power that will make it possible for you to persevere.* You have no doubt heard of the Keswick Convention, born out of the Moody-Sankey revival of 1875. The aim of this annual convention is to promote "practical holiness." The primary focus of the convention is that Christ is prepared to take upon himself the care and preservation of our lives every day and all day if we trust Him to do it. This truth is borne out in the testimonies given by many at the convention. Many have said that they felt called to a new surrender, to a complete consecration of their life to Christ, but they were hindered by a fear of failure. The thirst after holiness, after unbroken fellowship with Jesus, and after a life of persevering childlike obedience drew them in one direction. But the question always came up: "Will I continue to be faithful?" And to this question there came no answer until they believed that the surrender must be made not in their

own strength but in a power given them by the glorified Christ. He would not only keep them for the future, but He would also make possible the surrender of faith that expects future grace. It was in the power of Christ himself that they were able to present their lives to Him.

Oh, reader, believe it; a victorious life is possible. Christ, the Victor, is your Lord, who will undertake for you in everything and will enable you to do all that the Father expects of you. Be of good courage. Trust Him to do this great work for you, who has so freely given His life for you and forgiven you your sins. Only be bold to surrender yourself to a life kept from sin by the power of God. Along with the deepest conviction that in you dwells no good thing, confess that you see in the Lord Jesus all the goodness you will ever need for the life of a child of God. Begin literally to live "by the faith of the Son of God, who loved you, and gave himself for you."

For your encouragement, I will share the testimony of Bishop Moule, a man of deep humility. When he first heard of the Keswick Convention, he was afraid of "perfectionism" and would have nothing to do with it. Unexpectedly, during a vacation in Scotland, he came in contact with some friends at a small convention. There he heard an address that convinced him how entirely the teaching was according to Scripture. There was no word about sinlessness in the flesh or in man. Rather, it was a word about how Jesus can keep a man with a sinful nature from practicing sin. The light dawned in his heart. He who had always been counted a sensitive, obedient Christian came in touch with a new experience of what Christ will do for the one who gives himself completely to Him.

Here is what Bishop Moule says about the text "I can do all things through Christ who strengthens me":

I dare to say that it is possible for those who really are willing to reckon on the power of the Lord, for keeping and victory, to lead a life in which His promises are taken as they stand, and are found to be true. It is possible to cast all our care on Him daily, and to enjoy deep peace in doing it. It is possible to have the thoughts and imaginations of our hearts purified in the deepest meaning of the word, through faith. It is possible to see the will of God in everything, and to receive it, not with sighing, but with singing. It is possible, in the inner life of desire and feeling, to lay aside all bitterness, and wrath, and anger, and evil speaking, every day and every hour. It is possible, by taking complete refuge in divine power, to become strong through and through; and where previously our greatest weakness lay, to find that the things which formerly upset all our resolves to be patient, or pure, or humble, furnish today an opportunity to make sin powerless—through Him who loved us, and works in us an agreement with His will, and a blessed sense of His presence and His power. These things are divine possibilities, and because they are His work, the true experience of them will always cause us to bow lower at His feet, and to learn to thirst and long for more. We cannot possibly be satisfied with anything less than to walk with God—each day, each hour, each moment, in Christ, through the power of the Holy Spirit.

Thank God, a life of victory is sure for those who have a knowledge of their inward ruin and are hopeless in themselves but who, in "the confidence of despair," have looked to Jesus. They, in faith in His power to make the act of surrender possible for them, have done it in His might and now rely on Him alone every day and every hour.

Part Two

The Inner Room

Chapter 14

Suggestions for Private Prayer

A brother who had earnestly confessed his neglect of prayer but who was later able to declare that his eyes had been opened to see that the Lord supplies grace for all that He requires of us, asked if some suggestions could be given for spending the most profitable time in private prayer. Since the question came after a conference, and there was no opportunity then to give him a sufficient answer, I will share the following now in the hope that it will be of help to some:

1. As you enter a time of private prayer, let your first focus be to give thanks to God for the unspeakable love that invites you to come to Him and to converse freely with Him. If your heart is cold and dead, remember that your faith is not a matter of feeling but first involves the will. Raise your heart to God and thank Him for the assurance you have that He looks down on you and will bless you. Through such an act of faith you honor God and draw your soul away from being occupied with itself. Think also of the glorious grace of the Lord Jesus, who is willing to teach you to pray and to give you the disposition to do so. Think too of the Holy

Spirit, who was given to enable you to cry, "Abba, Father" in your heart and to help your faltering prayer. Five minutes spent in this way will strengthen your faith. Once more I say: Begin with an act of thanksgiving, and praise God for your place of prayer and the promise of blessing there.

2. You must prepare yourself for prayer by Bible study. The first reason why the quiet time is not attractive to most is that people do not know how to pray. Their storehouse of words is soon exhausted, and they do not know what else to say, because they forget that prayer is not a soliloquy, where everything comes from one side; it is a dialogue, where God's child listens to what the Father says, replies to it, and then makes his requests known.

Read a few verses from the Bible. Do not concern yourself with the difficulties contained in them. You can consider these later; but take what you do understand, apply it to yourself, and ask the Father to make His Word light and power in your heart. In this way you will have material enough for prayer from the Word; you will also have the liberty to ask for things you need. Keep on in this way, and the prayer room will become at length not a place where you sigh and struggle, but one of living fellowship with the Father in heaven. Prayerful study of the Bible is indispensable for powerful prayer.

3. When you have thus received the Word into your heart, turn to serious prayer. But do not attempt it hastily or thoughtlessly, as though you knew well enough how to pray on your own. Prayer in our own strength brings no blessing. Take time to present yourself reverently and in quietness before God. Remember His greatness and holiness and love. Think over what you want to ask of Him. Do not be satisfied with going over the same things every day. No child goes on

saying the same thing day after day to his earthly father.

What you talk about with the Father is influenced by the needs of the day. Let your prayer be something definite, arising either out of the Word that you have read or out of the real spiritual needs that you long to have satisfied. Let your prayer be so definite that you can say as you go out, "I know what I have asked of my Father, and I expect an answer." It is a good idea to sometimes take a piece of paper and write down what you will pray for.

4. What has been said is in reference to your own needs. But you know that we are encouraged to pray for the needs of others and how we may help them. One of the main reasons why daily prayer does not bring more joy and blessing is that it is basically selfish. Selfishness is the death of prayer.

Remember your family; your church with its many interests and endeavors; your own neighborhood; your friends. Let your heart be enlarged and take up the interests of missions and of the church throughout the world. Become an intercessor, and you will experience for the first time the blessedness of being used of God to bless others through prayer. You will begin to feel that there is something worth living for as you see that you have something to say to God. You will find that He will do things in answer to your prayers that otherwise would not have been done.

A child can ask his father for his basic needs. A full-grown son converses with him about his business and family responsibilities. A weak child of God prays only for himself; a full-grown man in Christ understands how to consult with God over what must take place in the kingdom. Let your prayer list bear the names of those for whom you pray—your minister, other ministers in the community, and missionary affairs with which you are familiar. Thus the inner room will become a wonder of God's goodness and a fountain of great joy. It can become the most blessed place on earth. It may be hard to believe, but it is the simple truth that God will make it a Bethel, where His angels ascend and descend, and where you will cry out, "The Lord shall be my God!" He will make it a Peniel, where you will see the face of God, as a prince of God, as one who wrestled with the angel and overcame him.

5. Do not forget the close bond between the inner room and the outside world. The attitude of the inner prayer room must remain with us all day. The object of secret prayer is to unite us to God that we may know His abiding presence with us. Sin, thoughtlessness, yielding to the flesh or the world, makes us unfit for prayer and casts a cloud over our soul. If you have stumbled or fallen, return to your secret place; let your first task be to invoke the blood of Jesus and to claim its cleansing power. Do not rest until you have fully confessed, repented of, and put away your sin. Let the precious blood of Jesus give you a fresh freedom of approach to God. Remember that the roots of your life in the inner room reach far out through body and soul so as to manifest themselves in all of life. Let "the obedience of faith," in which you pray in secret, rule you constantly. The inner room is intended to bind man to God, to supply him with power from God, and to enable him to live for God alone. Thank God for that place and for the blessed life that He will enable you there to experience and nourish.

Chapter 15

The Use of Time and the Example of Paul

Before the creation of the world, time did not exist. God lived in eternity in a way that we little understand. With creation, time began, and everything was placed under its power. God has placed all living creatures under a law of slow growth. Think of the length of time it takes for a child to become a man in body and mind. In learning, in wisdom, in business, in leisure work, and in politics, everything somehow depends on patience and perseverance. Everything needs time.

It is the same in religion. There can be no dialogue with a holy God, no fellowship between heaven and earth, no power for the salvation of the souls of others, unless time is set apart for it. Just as it is necessary for a child to eat in order to grow and to learn every day for many years to develop his mind, so the life of grace entirely depends on the time we are willing to give to it day by day.

A minister of the gospel is appointed by God to teach and help those who are engaged in ordinary occupations of life to find sufficient time and use it correctly for the preservation of his spiritual life. Of course, the minister cannot do this unless he has a living experience of a life of prayer. His highest calling is not preaching, or speaking, or church visitation, but it is to *cultivate the life of God in himself daily,* and to be a *witness of what the Lord teaches him* and accomplishes in him.

It was true even of the Lord Jesus. Why was it necessary that He who had no sin to confess sometimes spent all night in prayer to God? It is because his spiritual life had to be strengthened through an intimate relationship with His Father. His experience of a life in which He took time for fellowship with God enabled Him to share that life with us.

I pray that each minister of the gospel might understand that he has received this precious space of time from God in order to wait on Him! God must have for fellowship with himself the first and the best of our time. Without this, our preaching and our service will have little power. Here on earth I may expend my time in exchange for money or learning. The minister exchanges his time for divine power and the spiritual blessings to be obtained from heaven. That, and nothing else, makes him a man of God and ensures that his preaching will be in the demonstration of the Spirit and power.

"Follow my example, as I follow the example of Christ" (1 Corinthians 11:1).

Paul was a minister who prayed much for his congregation. Read his words prayerfully so that you may hear the voice of the Spirit.

"Night and day we pray most earnestly that we may see you again and supply what is lacking in your faith. Now may our God and Father himself and our Lord Jesus clear the way for us to come to you. May the Lord make your love increase and overflow for each other and for everyone else, just as ours does for you. May he strengthen your hearts so that you will be blameless and holy in the presence of our God and Father when our Lord Jesus comes with all his holy ones" (1 Thessalonians 3:10–13).

"May God himself, the God of peace, sanctify you through and through. May your whole spirit, soul and body be kept blameless at the coming of our Lord Jesus Christ" (1 Thessalonians 5:23).

What food for meditation!

"May our Lord Jesus Christ himself and God our Father, who loved us and by his grace gave us eternal encouragement and good hope, encourage your hearts and strengthen you in every good deed and word" (2 Thessalonians 2:16–17).

"God, whom I serve with my whole heart in preaching the gospel of his Son, is my witness how constantly I remember you in my prayers at all times; and I pray that now at last by God's will the way may be opened for me to come to you. I long to see you so that I may impart to you some spiritual gift to make you strong" (Romans 1:9–11).

"Brothers, my heart's desire and prayer to God for the Israelites is that they may be saved" (Romans 10:1).

"For this reason, ever since I heard about your faith in the Lord Jesus and your love for all the saints, I have not stopped giving thanks for you, remembering you in my prayers. I keep asking that the God of our Lord Jesus Christ, the glorious Father, may give you the Spirit of wisdom and revelation, so that you may know him better. I pray also that the eyes of your heart may be enlightened in order that you may know the hope to which he has called you, the riches of his glorious inheritance in the saints, and his incomparably great power for us who believe. That power is like the working of his mighty strength" (Ephesians 1:15–19).

"For this reason I kneel before the Father, from whom his whole family in heaven and on earth derives its name. I pray that out of his glorious riches he may strengthen you with power through his Spirit in your inner being, so that Christ may dwell in your hearts through faith. And I pray that you, being rooted and established in love, may have power, together with all the saints, to grasp how wide and long and high and deep is the love of Christ, and to know this love that surpasses knowledge—that you may be filled to the measure of all the fullness of God" (Ephesians 3:14–19).

"In all my prayers for all of you, I always pray with joy because of your partnership in the gospel from the first day until now, being confident of this, that he who began a good work in you will carry it on to completion until the day of Christ Jesus. It is right for me to feel this way about all of you, since I have you in my heart; for whether I am in chains or defending and confirming the gospel, all of you share in God's grace with me. God can testify how I long for all of you with the affection of Christ Jesus. And this is my prayer: that your love may abound more and more in knowledge and depth of insight, so that you may be able to discern what is best and may be pure and blameless until the day of Christ, filled with the fruit of righteousness that comes through Jesus Christ—to the glory and praise of God" (Philippians 1:4–11).

"And my God will meet all your needs according to his glorious riches in Christ Jesus" (Philippians 4:19).

"For this reason, since the day we heard about you, we have not stopped praying for you and asking God to fill you

with the knowledge of his will through all spiritual wisdom and understanding. And we pray this in order that you may live a life worthy of the Lord and may please him in every way: bearing fruit in every good work, growing in the knowledge of God, being strengthened with all power according to his glorious might so that you may have great endurance and patience" (Colossians 1:9–11).

"I want you to know how much I am struggling for you and for those at Laodicea, and for all who have not met me personally. My purpose is that they may be encouraged in heart and united in love, so that they may have the full riches of complete understanding, in order that they may know the mystery of God, namely, Christ" (Colossians 2:1–2).

This incredible study for our private prayer time teaches us that unceasing prayer formed a large part of Paul's service in the gospel. We see the high spiritual aim that he set before himself in his work on behalf of believers, and the tender and self-sacrificing love with which he always thought of the church body and its needs. Let us ask God to bring each one of us and all ministers of His Word to a life of which such prayer is the healthy and natural outflow. We will need to turn again and again to these pages if we would be brought by the Spirit to the apostolic life given to us here by God as an example.

Not only did Paul pray much for his congregation but he also asked his congregation to pray. Read again with prayerful attention:

"I urge you, brothers, by our Lord Jesus Christ and by the love of the Spirit, to join me in my struggle by praying to God for me. Pray that I may be rescued from the unbelievers in Judea and that my service in Jerusalem may be acceptable to the saints there" (Romans 15:30–31).

"Indeed, in our hearts we felt the sentence of death. But this happened that we might not rely on ourselves but on God, who raises the dead. He has delivered us from such a deadly peril, and he will deliver us. On him we have set our hope that he will continue to deliver us, as you help us by your prayers. Then many will give thanks on our behalf for the gracious favor granted us in answer to the prayers of many" (2 Corinthians 1:9–11).

"And pray in the Spirit on all occasions with all kinds of prayers and requests. With this in mind, be alert and always keep on praying for all the saints. Pray also for me, that whenever I open my mouth, words may be given me so that I will fearlessly make known the mystery of the gospel, for which I am an ambassador in chains. Pray that I may declare it fearlessly, as I should" (Ephesians 6:18–20).

"For I know that through your prayers and the help given by the Spirit of Jesus Christ, what has happened to me will turn out for my deliverance. I eagerly expect and hope that I will in no way be ashamed, but will have sufficient courage so that now as always Christ will be exalted in my body, whether by life or by death" (Philippians 1:19).

"Devote yourselves to prayer, being watchful and thankful. And pray for us, too, that God may open a door for our message, so that we may proclaim the mystery of Christ, for which I am in chains. Pray that I may proclaim it clearly, as I should" (Colossians 4:2–4).

"Finally, brothers, pray for us that the message of the Lord may spread rapidly and be honored, just as it was with you" (2 Thessalonians 3:1).

What a deep insight Paul had as to the unity of the body of Christ and the relationship of its members one to another! As we permit the Holy Spirit to work in us, He will reveal

this truth to us as well. What a glimpse Paul gives us of the power of the spiritual life among these Christians by the way in which he knew that at Rome, Corinth, Ephesus, Colosse, and Philippi, there were men and women on whom he could rely for prayer because they had power with God! What a lesson for all ministers of the gospel, to lead them to inquire if they truly appreciate the unity of the body at its true value; ask if they are endeavoring to train up Christians as intercessors. Ask if they understand that the reason Paul had that confidence was because he himself was so strong in prayer for the congregation. Let us together learn the lesson, and seek God that we all may grow in the grace of prayer, so that all our service and Christian life may witness that the Spirit of prayer rules us. May we have confidence that God will avenge His own elect that cry out to Him day and night.

Chapter 16

Ministers of the Spirit

What is the meaning of the expression "The minister of the gospel is a minister of the Spirit"? (See 2 Corinthians 3:6–8.) It means:

1. The preacher is entirely under the power and control of the Holy Spirit, so that he may be led and used by the Spirit as He wills.

2. Many pray for the Spirit that they may make use of Him and His power for their work. This is an entirely wrong concept. It is He who must use you. Your relationship toward Him must be one of deep dependence and utter submission. The Spirit must have you completely and always and in all things under His power.

3. There are many who think they must only preach the Word, and that the Spirit will make the Word fruitful. They do not understand that it is the Spirit, in and through the preacher, who will bring the Word to the heart of the listeners. I must not be satisfied with praying to God to bless through the operation of His Spirit the Word that I preach. The Lord wants me to be filled with the Spirit; then I will speak as I should and my preaching will be in the manifestation of the Spirit and power.

4. We see this occurring on the day of Pentecost. They

were filled with the Spirit and began to speak, and spoke with power through the Spirit who was in them.

5. Thus we learn what the relationship of the minister toward the Spirit should be. He must have a strong belief that the Spirit is in him, that the Spirit will teach him in his daily life, and that He will strengthen him to bear witness to the Lord Jesus in his preaching and visiting. He must live in ceaseless prayer that he may be kept and strengthened by the power of the Spirit.

6. When the Lord promised the apostles that they would receive power when the Holy Spirit came upon them, and commanded them to wait for Him, it was as though He said: "Do not dare to preach without this power. It is the indispensable preparation for your work. Everything depends on it."

7. What is the lesson to be learned from the phrase "ministers of the Spirit"? How little we have understood this! How little we have lived in it! How little we have experienced the power of the Holy Spirit! What must we do? There must be deep confession that we have indeed grieved the Spirit, because we have not lived daily in dependence upon Him. There must be simple, childlike surrender to His leading, in the confidence that the Lord will work a change in us. Then there must be daily fellowship with the Lord Jesus in ceaseless prayer. He will bestow on us the Holy Spirit like rivers of living water.

Little time in the Word together with little prayer is death to the spiritual life. Much of the Word but little prayer yields a less than healthy spiritual life. Time spent in prayer with little time in the Word yields life, but without steadfastness. A full measure of the Word and much prayer each day produces a healthy and powerful life. Think of the Lord Jesus. In His youth and through to adulthood He treasured the Word in His heart. He showed that the Word of God filled His heart when he was tempted in the wilderness, as well as at every opportunity that presented itself—until He cried out on the cross in death: "My God, my God, why have you forsaken me?"

In His prayer life He manifested two things. First, He showed that the Word supplies us with material for prayer and encourages us to expect everything from God. The second is that it is only by prayer that we may live such a life that every word of God might be fulfilled in us. How can we come to the point where the Word and prayer each have their undivided right over us? There is only one answer. Our lives must be wholly transformed. We must get a new, healthy, heavenly life, in which hunger after God's Word and thirst after God himself are expressed in prayer as naturally as the needs of our earthly life. Every manifestation of the power of the flesh in us and the weakness of our spiritual life must drive us to the conviction that God, through the powerful operation of His Holy Spirit, will work out a new and strong life in us.

We must understand that the Holy Spirit is essentially the Spirit of the Word and the Spirit of prayer. He will cause the Word to become joy and light in our souls. He will also help us in prayer to know the mind and will of God and to find in it our delight. If we wish to explain these things to God's people that they may know the inheritance that is prepared for them, we must commit ourselves from this moment forward to the leading of the Holy Spirit. We must through faith in what He will do in us appropriate the heavenly life of Christ as He lived it on earth, with certain expectation that the Spirit who filled Him with the Word and prayer will also accomplish that work in us.

Let us believe that the Spirit who is in us is the Spirit of the Lord Jesus and that He is in us to make us truly partakers of His life. If we firmly believe this and set our hearts upon it, there will come a change in our involvement with the Word and prayer such as we could not have thought possible. Believe it firmly and expect it.

Chapter 17

Preaching and Prayer

We are familiar with the vision of the valley of dry bones. We know that the Lord said to the prophet Ezekiel: "Prophesy to these bones and say to them, 'Dry bones, hear the word of the Lord!' This is what the Sovereign Lord says to these bones: I will make breath enter you, and you will come to life" (Ezekiel 37:4–5). When he had done this, there was a noise, and bone came together to its bone, and flesh came up, and skin covered them—but there was no breath in them. The prophesying to the bones—the preaching of the Word of God—had a powerful influence. It was the beginning of the great miracle that was about to happen, and there lay an entire army of men newly made. It was the beginning of the work of life in them, but there was no spirit there.

Then he said to me, "Prophesy to the breath; prophesy, son of man, and say to it, 'This is what the Sovereign Lord says: Come from the four winds, O breath, and breathe into these slain, that they may live'." (v. 9). When the prophet had done this, the Spirit came upon them, and they lived and stood on their feet, a very great army. Prophesying to the bones, that is, preaching, has accomplished a great work. There lay the beautiful new bodies. But prophesying to the Spirit: "Come, O Spirit," that is prayer, and that has accomplished a far more wonderful thing. The power of the Spirit was revealed through prayer.

Is not the work of our preachers and ministers mostly prophesying to dry bones, making known the promises of God? This is sometimes followed by great results. Everything that belongs to the form of godliness has been done to perfection; a careless congregation becomes regular and devout, but it remains true for the most part that "there is no life in them." Preaching must always be followed up by prayer. The preacher must come to see that his preaching is comparatively powerless to bring new life until he begins to take time for prayer, and according to the teaching of God's Word, he strives and labors and continues in prayer; and he takes no rest and gives God no rest until He bestows the Spirit in overflowing power.

Do you agree that a change must be seen in our work? We must learn from Peter to continue in prayer for the ministry of the Word. Just as we are zealous preachers, we must be zealous in prayer. We must with all our strength, and as consistently as Paul did, pray unceasingly. For the prayer: "Come, breathe on these slain," the answer is certain.

Chapter 18

Wholeheartedness

Experience teaches us that anyone who engages in a work less than wholeheartedly will seldom succeed. Imagine a student, or his teacher, a man of business, or a warrior, who does not give himself to the task at hand. That one cannot expect success.

Wholeheartedness is even more essential in spiritual work, and above all, of the high and holy task of prayer and of being always well pleasing to a holy God. We are reminded of this in Jeremiah: "You will seek me and find me when you seek me with all your heart" (29:13).

Many of God's servants have said at one time or another, "I seek God with my whole heart"—but have you ever thought how many Christians there are of whom it is all too plain that they do *not* seek God with their whole heart? When in despair over their sins, they seem to seek God wholeheartedly. But once they know His forgiveness, even though they may display some Christian virtue, it would be difficult to say of them, "This man has surrendered his whole heart to follow God and to serve Him as the supreme effort of his life."

How is it with you? What does your heart tell you? Even though you have given yourself to fulfill your obligations faithfully and zealously (even as a minister), perhaps you need to acknowledge: "I am convinced that the reason for my unsatisfactory prayer life is that I have not lived with a wholehearted surrender of all that would hinder my fellowship with God." What a deeply important question to consider in our prayer time and then to give the answer to God! How vital to arrive at a clear answer, and to confess it all before God alone!

Prayerlessness is not something that can be overcome as an isolated thing. It is related to the state of the heart. And it is a way of life. True prayer depends on an undivided heart. And I cannot give myself an undivided heart—one that enables me to say, "I seek God with my whole heart." It is impossible for us in our own strength; but God will do it. He said He would give us a heart to fear Him. He also said He would write His law on our heart. Such promises serve to awaken a desire to pray. However weak our desire may be, if there is a sincere determination to strive after what God has for us, He will work in our heart both to will and to do of His good pleasure. It is the great work of the Holy Spirit in us to make us willing. He enables us to seek God with our whole heart. May we acknowledge that we have been doubleminded, because while we have given ourselves to many earthly things with all our heart and strength, we cannot always say that we have given ourselves to fellowship with God with our whole heart.

Chapter 19

"Follow Me"

The Lord did not say these words to all who believed on Him, or who hoped to be blessed by Him, but only to those whom He would make fishers of men. He said this not only when He first called the apostles but also later on to Peter: "Don't be afraid; from now on you will catch men" (Luke 5:10). The holy art of winning souls, of loving and saving them, can be learned only in a close and consistent relationship with Christ. What a lesson for ministers, Christian workers, and others! This intimate relationship was the great and particular privilege of His disciples. The Lord chose them that they might always be with Him and remain near Him. We read of the choice of the twelve apostles in Mark 3:14: "He appointed twelve . . . that they might be with him and that he might send them out to preach." And on the last night our Lord said, "And you also must testify, for you have been with me from the beginning" (John 15:27).

This fact was observed by outsiders. For instance, the girl who spoke to Peter after Jesus was taken away, said, "You also were with Jesus of Galilee" (Matthew 26:69). And the Sanhedrin, when they saw the courage of Peter and John: "They were astonished and they took note that these men had been with Jesus" (Acts 4:13).

The chief characteristic and indispensable qualification for the one who would bear witness to Christ is that he spend time in His presence.

Continuous fellowship with Christ is the only school for the training of students of the Holy Spirit. What a lesson for us all! Only he who, like Caleb, follows the Lord fully will have power to teach other souls the art of following Jesus. But what an amazing grace, that the Lord Jesus himself wants to train us to be like Him so that others may learn from us. Then we will be able to say with Paul: "Follow my example, as I follow the example of Christ" (1 Corinthians 11:1).

Never has a teacher taken such trouble with his scholars as Jesus Christ will with those who preach His Word. He will spare no pain; no time will be too limited or too long for Him. In the love that took Him to the cross, He wants to fellowship and converse with us, fashion us, sanctify us, and make us fit for His holy service. Dare we still complain that it is too much for us to spend so much time in prayer? Will we not commit ourselves entirely to the love that gave up all for us and look upon it as our greatest joy to have daily fellowship with Him? All you who long for blessing in your ministry, He calls you to abide in Him. Let it be the greatest delight of your life to spend time with God; it will be the surest preparation for fruitful service.

Lord, draw me, help me, hold me fast. Day by day teach me how to live by faith in your sweet fellowship.

Chapter 20

The Holy Trinity

God is an ever-flowing fountain of pure love and blessedness. Christ is the reservoir wherein the fullness of God was
made visible as grace, and has been opened for us. The Holy
Spirit is the stream of living water that flows from under the
throne of God and of the Lamb.

The Redeemed, God's believing children, are the channels
through which the love of the Father, the grace of Christ, and
the powerful operation of the Spirit are brought to earth to
be imparted to others.

What a clear picture we get here of the wonderful partnership in which God includes us as dispensers of the grace
of God! The time we spend in prayer covering our own
needs is only the beginning of the life of prayer. The glory of
prayer is that we have power as intercessors to bring the
grace of Christ and the energizing power of the Spirit upon
those souls that are still in darkness.

The more closely the channel is connected with the reservoir, the more certainly will the water flow unhindered
through it. The more we are occupied in prayer with the fullness of Christ and the Spirit who proceeds from Him, the
more firmly will we abide in fellowship with Him, and the
more surely will our lives be full of joy and strength. This,

however, is still only a preparation for the real work of prayer. The more we yield ourselves to fellowship with the triune God, the sooner we will gain the courage and ability to intercede for others in our families, in our neighborhoods, and in our churches.

Are we truly channels that remain open, so that water may flow through to the thirsty, lost souls in a dry, barren land? Have you offered yourself without reservation to God, to become a bearer of the energizing operation of the Holy Spirit?

Perhaps the reason we do not experience the full power of prayer is because we think so much of our own needs and of ourselves. We must understand that the new prayer life to which we have been called by the Lord Jesus can be sustained and strengthened only through the intercession through which we labor for the souls around us in order to bring them to know the Lord.

Meditate on this: God is an ever-flowing fountain of love and blessing, and I, as His child, am a living channel through which the Spirit and His life can be brought to earth every day!

Chapter 21

Life and Prayer

Our daily life has a tremendous influence on our prayers, just as our prayers influence our daily life. In fact, our life is a continuous prayer. We are continually praising or thanking God by our actions and by the manner in which we treat others. This natural prayer and desire for God can be so strong in a man (who also prays to God) that the words of prayer that he actually utters cannot be heard. At times God cannot hear the prayer of your lips, because the worldly desires of your heart cry out to Him much more strongly and loudly.

As we have said, life exercises a mighty influence over prayer. A worldly life or a self-seeking life, for example, makes prayer by that person powerless and an answer impossible. With many Christians there is conflict between their everyday life and their prayer life, and the everyday life holds the upper hand. But as we have said, prayer can also exercise a strong influence over our everyday life. If I yield myself completely to God in prayer, prayer can overcome a life in the flesh and the practice of sin. The entire life may be brought under the control of prayer. Prayer can change and renew the life, because prayer calls upon and receives the Lord Jesus, and the Holy Spirit purifies and sanctifies us.

Because of their defective spiritual life, many people think they must make a supreme effort in order to pray more. They do not understand, of course, that only in proportion as the spiritual life is strengthened can the prayer life increase. Prayer and life are inseparably connected and the quality of each deeply related.

What do you think? Which has the stronger influence over you: five- or ten-minute prayers, or the whole day spent thinking on worldly desires? Do not be surprised if your prayers are not answered. The reason may easily be that your life and your prayers work against each other; your heart concentrates more on living than on praying. Learn this great lesson: My prayer must rule my whole life. What I request from God in prayer is not decided in five or ten minutes. I must learn to say: "I have prayed with my whole heart." What I desire from God must truly fill my heart the whole day; then the way is opened for a definite answer.

How sacred and powerful prayer is when it takes possession of the heart and life! It keeps one constantly in fellowship with God. Then we can literally say, *I wait on you, Lord, all day long.* Let us be careful to consider not only the length of time we spend with God in prayer but also the power prayer has to take possession of our whole life.

The Twelve said, "It would not be right for us to neglect the ministry of the word of God in order to wait on tables" (Acts 6:2). For that work deacons were chosen. And this word of the disciples serves for all time and for all who are set apart as ministers. "We will turn this responsibility over to them and will give our attention to prayer and the ministry of the word" (v. 3). Dr. Alexander Whyte once said, "I think sometimes, when my salary is paid to me so faithfully and punctually: the deacons have performed faithfully their part of the agreement; have I been just as faithful in my part, in persevering in prayer and the ministry of the Word?" Another minister said, "How surprised people would be if I proposed to divide my time between these two equally—one half given to prayer and the other to the ministry of the Word."

In the case of Peter, notice what perseverance in prayer meant. He went up on the roof to pray. There, in prayer, he received heavenly instruction as to his work among the heathen. There, the message from Cornelius came to him. There, the Holy Spirit told him to rise and go with the three men who sought him. From there he went to Caesarea, where the Spirit was unexpectedly poured out on the heathen. All this is to teach us that it is through prayer that God will give the instruction of His Spirit to enable us to understand His will, to let us know with whom we are to speak, and to give us the assurance that His Spirit will make His Word effective through us.

As a minister of the gospel, have you ever considered why you have a salary and a place to live, and so are freed from the need of holding a regular job? The reason is so that you can continue in prayer and the ministry of the Word. These will give you the necessary wisdom and anointing for your work. And that is the secret of a fruitful ministry.

No wonder there are often complaints about the ineffective spiritual life of a minister and his congregation. That which is of prime importance—perseverance in prayer—does not occupy its rightful place.

Peter was able to speak and act as he did because he was filled with the Spirit. Let us not be satisfied with anything less than full surrender to and undivided appropriation of the Spirit, as leader and Lord of our lives. Nothing less will empower us. Then, for the first time, we will be able to say, "God has made us able ministers of His Spirit."

Chapter 22

Are We Carnal or
Spiritual?

There is a great difference between being carnal [living after the flesh] and being spiritual. This fact is little understood or pondered. The Christian who walks in the Spirit, and has crucified the flesh, is spiritual (Galatians 5:24). The Christian who walks after the flesh, and wishes to please the flesh, is carnal (Romans 13:14). The Galatians, who had begun in the Spirit, reverted to a life in the flesh. Yet there were among them some spiritual members, who were able to restore the wandering with true meekness.

What a difference between the carnal and the spiritual Christian (1 Corinthians 3:1–3)! With the carnal Christian, there may be the appearance of virtue and zeal for God and His service, but it is for the most part a manifestation of human power. With the spiritual Christian, on the other hand, there is a complete submission to the leading of the Spirit, a sense of personal weakness and total dependence on the work of Christ—it is a life of abiding fellowship with Christ brought into being by the Spirit.

How important it is for us to discover and to clearly

acknowledge before God whether we are spiritual or carnal. A minister may be very faithful in his teaching of doctrine and be enthusiastic in his service, and yet be so, for the most part, in the power of human wisdom and zeal. One of the signs of this is little pleasure or perseverance in fellowship with Christ through prayer. A love of prayer is one of the marks of the Spirit.

A tremendous change is in store for the carnal Christian who would become truly spiritual. At first he cannot understand what needs to change or how it will take place. But the more the truth dawns upon him, the more he is convinced that it is impossible unless God does the work. Yet to believe that God will do it requires diligent prayer. Meditation and a quiet, solitary place are indispensable, along with the end of all confidence in self. But along this road there comes the faith that God is willing, and He will do it.

How can you say to others: "Brothers, I could not address you as spiritual but as worldly—mere infants in Christ" (1 Corinthians 3:1) unless you yourself have the experience of having passed from the one state to the other? But God will teach you. Persevere in prayer and in faith.

Chapter 23

Examples in Godly Men

George Müller

Just as God gave the apostle Paul as an example in his prayer life for Christians of all time, so in more recent times He has given George Müller as proof to His church how literally and wonderfully He still hears and answers prayer. Not only did God give this man of God over a million pounds sterling in his lifetime to support his orphanages, but Müller also stated that he believed the Lord had given him more than thirty thousand souls in answer to prayer. These were not only from among the orphans but also many others for whom he had prayed faithfully every day (in some cases for fifty years), in the firm faith that they would be saved. When he was asked on what ground he so firmly believed this, his answer was: "There are five conditions that I always endeavor to fulfill. In observing these, I have the assurance of an answer to my prayer:

1. "I have not the least doubt because I am assured that it is the Lord's will to save them, for He wills that all men should be saved, and come to the knowledge of the truth

(1 Timothy 2:4). Also, we have the assurance 'that if we ask any thing according to his will, he hears us' (1 John 5:14).

2. "I have never pleaded for their salvation in my own name, but in the blessed name of my precious Lord Jesus, and on His merits alone (John 14:14).

3. "I always firmly believed in the willingness of God to hear my prayers (Mark 11:24).

4. "I am not conscious of having yielded to any sin, for 'if I regard iniquity in my heart, the Lord will not hear me' when I call (Psalm 66:18).

5. "I have persevered in believing prayer for more than fifty-two years for some, and shall continue till the answer comes: 'Shall not God avenge his own elect, which cry day and night unto him?'"

Take these thoughts to heart and pray according to these rules. Let prayer be not only the utterance of your desires but also fellowship with God, until you know by faith that your prayer is heard. The way George Müller walked is the new and living way to the throne of grace, *which is open to all of us.*

Hudson Taylor

When as a young man Hudson Taylor surrendered unreservedly to the Lord, he received a strong conviction that God would send him to China. He had read of George Müller, and how God had answered his prayers for his own support and that of his orphans. Taylor began to ask the Lord to teach him also to trust God in the same way. But he felt that if he wanted to go to China with such faith, he must first begin in England to live by faith. He asked the Lord to enable him to do this. He worked as a doctor's assistant, and asked God to help him not to ask for his salary, but to leave

it to God to move the heart of the doctor to pay him at the right time. The doctor was a goodhearted man, but very irregular in payment. This cost Taylor much trouble and struggle in prayer because he believed, like George Müller, that the word "Owe no man anything" was to be taken literally, and that debt should not be incurred.

So he learned to move men through God—a profound lesson, which later became an unspeakably great blessing to him in his work in China. He believed that we should—in the conversion of the Chinese, in the awakening of Christians to give money for the support of the work, and in the finding of suitable missionaries who would keep this as faith's rule of conduct—make our desires known to God in prayer, and then rely on God to move men to do what He would have done.

After some years in China, he prayed that God would provide twenty-four missionaries, two for each of the eleven provinces, and two for Mongolia, each with millions of souls and no missionary. God did it. But there was no society to send them out. He had indeed learned to trust God for his own support, but he dared not take upon himself the responsibility of the twenty-four. He feared they might not have sufficient faith. This caused him severe conflict, and he became very ill under it, until at last he saw that God could just as easily care for the twenty-four as for himself. Then he assumed this responsibility in glad faith. And so God led him, through many severe trials of faith, to trust Him fully. These twenty-four increased in course of time to one thousand missionaries who relied wholly on God for support. Other missionary societies have acknowledged how much they learned from Hudson Taylor as a man who stated and obeyed this law: "Faith may rely on God to move men to do what His children have asked of Him in prayer."

Chapter 24

Light From the Inner Room

"But when you pray, go into your room, close the door and pray to your Father, who is unseen. Then your Father, who sees what is done in secret, will reward you" (Matthew 6:6).

Our Lord spoke of the prayer of the hypocrites who desire to be seen of men, and also of the prayer of the heathen who trust in their many words. They do not understand that prayer has no value except when addressed to a personal God who sees and hears. In the text, our Lord teaches a wonderful lesson concerning the inestimable blessing a Christian can have in his secret place of prayer. To understand the lesson fully, let us look at the light the prayer room sheds on:

1. *The wonderful love of God.* Think of God, His greatness, His holiness, His unspeakable glory, and then imagine the inestimable privilege to which He invites His children, that each one of them, no matter how sinful or frail, may have access to God anytime and may talk with Him as long as he wishes. God is ready to meet His child anytime he enters his prayer room; He is ready to have fellowship with him, to give him the joy and strength that he needs along with the assurance that God is with him and will undertake for him in everything. In addition, God promises that He will enrich His child in his outward life and work with those things he has asked for in secret. We ought to cry out with

joy. What an honor! What a salvation!

Do you see what a generous supply He offers for every need? One may be in great distress or have fallen into deep sin. Or he may in the ordinary course of life desire temporal or spiritual blessings. Perhaps he wants to pray for himself or for his family, or for his congregation or denomination. He may even want to become an intercessor for the whole world—the promise for private prayer covers all: "Pray to your Father, who is unseen . . . your Father . . . will reward you openly."

We might well imagine that no place on earth would be so attractive to the child of God as the prayer room, where the presence of God is promised and unhindered fellowship with the Father awaits. Think about the happiness of a child on earth who enjoys the love of his father, the gratefulness of a friend who meets a beloved benefactor, or the thrill of a subject who has free access to his king and may stay with him as long as he wishes. All these joyful privileges are nothing compared with this heavenly promise. In your prayer room you can converse with God as long as you desire. You can rely on His presence and fellowship there.

Do you see the wonderful love of God in the gift of a prayer room sanctified by such a promise? Let us thank God every day of our lives for the gift of His wonderful love. In this sinful world, He could devise nothing more suitable for our needs than this fountain of unspeakable blessing.

2. *The deep sinfulness of man.* Perhaps we also imagine that every child of God takes advantage of such an invitation with joy. But what is the response? From everywhere the conclusion is reached that private, personal prayer is as a general rule neglected by those who call themselves believers. Many make *no* use of the privilege; they go to church, they

confess Christ, but they know little of personal fellowship with God. Many do pray, but in a spirit of haste, and more as a matter of custom or for the easing of conscience. They cannot really testify to any joy or blessing from it. What is worse, the many who know something of prayer's blessedness, confess that they know little about faithful, regular fellowship with the Father throughout the day as something that is as necessary as their daily bread.

What makes the prayer room so powerless? Is it not the sinfulness of man and his fallen nature's aversion to God, which make the world more attractive than being alone with the heavenly Father?

Do Christians truly believe the Word of God that declares that "the flesh is enmity against God"? Do they walk so much after the flesh that the Spirit cannot strengthen them for prayer? Do Christians allow Satan to deprive them of the use of the weapon of prayer so that they are powerless to overcome him? Our response only shows the deep sinfulness of man, because no greater proof exists than this: We neglect private prayer and so turn our backs on the love that gave us the privilege.

More disturbing is the fact that even ministers of the gospel acknowledge that they pray too little. The Word tells them that their only power lies in prayer: through it they can be clothed with power from on high for their work. But it seems that the power of the world and the flesh has distracted them. While they devote time to their work and manifest zeal in it, the most necessary thing of all is neglected, and there is no desire or strength for prayer to obtain the indispensable gift of the Holy Spirit to make their work fruitful. *God, give us grace to understand the deep sinfulness of our neglect of prayer.*

3. *The glorious grace of Christ Jesus.* Is there no hope of change? Must it be always so? Or is there a means of recovery? There is, thank God!

The man through whom God has made known the message of the inner room is none other than our Lord Jesus Christ, who saves us from our sins. He is able and willing to deliver us from this sin, and He will deliver us. He has not undertaken to redeem us from all our other sins and then leave us to deal with the sin of prayerlessness in our own strength. In this also we may come to Him and cry out, "Lord, if you will, you can make me clean. Lord, I believe; help my unbelief."

How can you experience this deliverance? By the well-known way by which every sinner must come to Christ: Begin by acknowledging and then confessing before Him, in a childlike manner, the sin of neglect of the place of prayer. Bow before Him in true repentance and sorrow. Tell Him that your heart has deceived you by the thought that you, in your own strength, could pray as you ought. Tell Him that through the weakness of the flesh, the power of the world, and self-confidence, you have been led astray, and that you have no strength to do better. Do this with your whole heart. By your own resolution and effort you cannot put things right.

In your sin and weakness come into your prayer room, and begin to thank God, as you have never thanked Him before, that the grace of the Lord Jesus will make it possible for you to converse with your Father as a child ought to. Once again, hand over to the Lord Jesus all your sin and misery, as well as your whole life and will, for Him to cleanse and take possession of as His own.

Even though your heart may be cold and dead, persevere

in the exercise of faith that Christ is an almighty and faithful Savior. You may be sure that deliverance will come. Expect it. You will begin to understand that the prayer room is the revelation of the glorious grace of the Lord Jesus, which makes it possible for one to do what he could not do by himself—maintain fellowship with God and receive the desire and power that equip a person for walking with God.

Part Three

The Deepest Secret of Pentecost

Chapter 25

The Spirit of the Cross in Our Lord

Sometimes we seek for the operation of the Spirit with the purpose of obtaining more power for work, more love in our life, more holiness in the heart, more light on Scripture or on our path. But all these gifts are subordinate to the great purpose of God. The Father bestowed the Spirit on the Son, and the Son gave Him to us for the purpose of revealing and glorifying Christ Jesus in us.

The heavenly Christ must become for us a real and living personality who is always with us and in us. Our life on earth can be lived every day in unbroken fellowship with our Lord Jesus. This is the first and greatest work of the Holy Spirit in the believer, that we should know and experience Christ as our life. God desires that we be strengthened with might by His Spirit in the inner man, so that Christ may dwell in our hearts through faith, so that we may be filled with all the fullness of God's love.

This was the secret of the joy of the first disciples. They had received the Lord Jesus—whom they feared they had lost—as the heavenly Christ into their hearts. And this was their preparation for Pentecost: their attention was completely taken up with Him. He was literally everything to them. Their hearts were empty of everything, so that the Spirit could fill them with Christ. In the fullness of the Spirit they had power for a life and service such as the Lord desired for them. Is this the goal of our desires and our experience? The Lord wants us to know that the blessing for which we have so diligently prayed can be increased in no other way than by the faithful cultivation of intimate fellowship with Christ in prayer every day.

It seems to me that there is a still deeper secret of Pentecost to be discovered. The thought has come to me that perhaps our concept of the Lord Jesus in heaven is too limited. We think of Him in the splendor and glory of God's throne. We also think of the incredible love that moved Him to give himself for us. But we forget that, above all, He was known here on earth as the Crucified One. In this capacity He has a place on the throne of God. "Then I saw a Lamb, looking as if it had been slain" (Revelation 5:6).

As the Crucified One, He is the object of the Father's eternal good pleasure and of the worship of the entire creation. It is, therefore, of prime importance that we on earth should know and experience Him as the Crucified One, so that we may manifest His disposition to others and share the power that can make them partakers of salvation.

I feel deeply that the cross is Christ's highest glory. The Holy Spirit neither has done nor can do anything greater or more glorious than He did when He "through the eternal Spirit offered himself unblemished to God" (Hebrews 9:14). Because of this, it is evident that the Holy Spirit can do nothing greater or more glorious for us than to bring us into the fellowship of that cross and work out in us the same spirit that was seen in our Lord Jesus. The question has come: "Is this the reason why our prayers for the powerful operation of the Holy Spirit cannot be answered? Have we sought too little to receive the Spirit who might help us to know and become like the glorified Christ in the fellowship of His cross?"

Is this the deepest secret of Pentecost? The Spirit comes to us from the cross, where He strengthened Christ to offer himself to God. He comes from the Father, who looked down with unspeakable good pleasure on the humiliation, obedience, and self-sacrifice of Christ as the highest proof of His surrender to Him. He comes from Christ, who through the cross was prepared to receive from the Father the fullness of the Spirit that He might share it with the world. He comes to reveal Christ to our hearts as the Lamb slain in the midst of the throne so that we on earth might worship Him as they do in heaven. He comes especially to impart to us the life of the crucified Christ so that we may be able to say, "I have been crucified with Christ and I no longer live, but Christ lives in me. The life I live in the body, I live by faith in the Son of God, who loved me and gave himself for me" (Galatians 2:20). To understand this secret, we must first meditate on the meaning and the value of the cross.

The cross is to be viewed from two standpoints.

First, from the standpoint of the work it accomplished: the pardon and conquest of sin. This is the first message communicated to the sinner from Mount Calvary. It proclaims free and full deliverance from the power of sin.

Second, from the standpoint of the disposition that was manifested on that rugged piece of wood. We find this amply expressed in Philippians 2:8: "And being found in appearance as a man, he humbled himself and became obedient to death—even death on a cross!" Here we see *self-abasement* to the lowest place that could be found under the burden of our sin and curse; *obedience* to the uttermost to all the will of God; and *self-sacrifice* to the death of the cross. These three words reveal to us the holy perfection of His person and work.

Therefore, God has greatly exalted Him. It was the spirit of the cross that made Him the object of His Father's good pleasure, of the worship of the angels, of the love and confidence of all the redeemed. The self-abasement of Christ, His obedience to the will of God even to death, and His self-sacrifice even to death on the cross—these identify Him as the Lamb John saw in the vision of Revelation: "looking as if it had been slain, standing in the center of the throne."

May the Holy Spirit reveal to us the disposition that was in Christ to submit himself to such agony and loss for our sake.

Chapter 26

The Spirit of the Cross in Us

All that Christ was and did was for us. And He desires to manifest in us that same spirit. The spirit of the cross was His blessedness and His glory. May it be for us also. He desires to duplicate His likeness in us and to give us a full share of all that is His.

Paul wrote, "Your attitude should be the same as that of Christ Jesus" (Philippians 2:5). Elsewhere he writes, "We have the mind of Christ" (1 Corinthians 2:16). We are exhorted in Romans 12:1: "Do not conform any longer to the pattern of this world, but be transformed by the renewing of your mind."

The fellowship of the cross is not only a holy duty for us, but an unspeakably blessed privilege, which the Holy Spirit himself makes ours according to the promises: "Everything that I learned from my Father I have made known to you" (John 15:15) and "When the Counselor comes, whom I will send to you from the Father, the Spirit of truth who goes out from the Father, he will testify about me. And you also must testify, for you have been with me from the beginning" (John 15:26–27).

The Holy Spirit formed this disposition in Christ, and He will also form it in us if we allow Him to.

When the Lord told His disciples that they must take up the cross and follow Him, from their frame of reference, they could hardly have understood His meaning. But He wanted to stir up their thinking, and so prepare them for the time when they would see Him carrying His cross. From the Jordan forward, where He had presented himself to be baptized and counted among sinners, He carried the cross in His heart. That is to say, He was always conscious that the sentence of death, because of sin, rested on Him, and that He must bear it to completion. As the disciples thought about this, and wondered what He meant, only one thing helped them to grasp it: In their day, carrying a cross was the language of a man who had been sentenced to death and must carry his cross to the appointed place.

About the same time, Christ had said, "Whoever finds his life will lose it, and whoever loses his life for my sake will find it" (Matthew 10:39). He taught them that they must despise their present life when compared to their life in Christ. Their nature was so sinful that nothing less than death could deliver them. Gradually the conviction dawned on them that the taking up of the cross meant: "I am to feel that my life is under sentence of death, and that under the consciousness of this sentence, I must constantly surrender my flesh and my sinful nature, even unto death."

So in a small sense they were prepared to see that the cross that Christ carried represented the power to deliver them from sin, and that they must first receive from Him the true spirit of the cross. From Him they would learn what self-humiliation in their weakness and unworthiness was to mean; what the obedience was that crucified their own will in all things, in the greatest as well as in the least; what the self-denial was that did not seek to please the flesh or the world.

"If anyone would come after me, he must deny himself and take up his cross and follow me" (Mark 8:34).

Chapter 27

We Are Crucified
With Christ

The lesson the Lord desired His disciples to learn from His statement concerning taking up their cross and losing their life finds its expression in the words Paul stated after Christ had died on the cross, was exalted on high, and the Spirit had been poured out: "I have been crucified with Christ and I no longer live, but Christ lives in me. May I never boast except in the cross of our Lord Jesus Christ, through which the world has been crucified to me, and I to the world" (Galatians 2:20; 6:14).

Paul wanted every believer to live a life that proved they were crucified with Christ. He wanted us to understand that the Christ who comes to dwell in our hearts is the Crucified One, who will impart to us the true mind of the cross. He tells us that "our old self was crucified with him" and that "anyone who has died has been freed from sin" (Romans 6:6–7). When believers receive by faith the crucified Christ, they in effect give their flesh over to the death sentence that was executed to the full on Calvary. Paul says, "If we have been united with him like this in his death, we will certainly also be united with him in his resurrection" (Romans 6:5), and, therefore, we must reckon that we are dead to sin in Christ Jesus.

These words of the Holy Spirit, through Paul, teach us that we must abide in the constant fellowship of the cross, in union with the crucified and now living Lord Jesus. It is the soul that lives under the cover and shelter and deliverance of the cross that alone can expect to experience the resurrection power of the Lord and His abiding presence.

There are many who place their hope of salvation in the redemption of the cross who understand little about the fellowship of the cross. These rely on what the cross purchased for them—the forgiveness of sins and peace with God—but seek to survive for long periods of time without fellowship with the Lord.

This is a tragedy.

Many do not know what it means to seek every day after heart communion with the crucified Lord as He is in heaven—"The Lamb in the midst of the throne." How wonderful if this vision of Christ could exercise its spiritual power upon us, that we might truly experience His presence with us every day here on earth!

You may ask, "Is it possible?" Without a doubt. Why was the Holy Spirit sent from heaven if it were not to make the presence of the glorified Jesus real to us on earth?

Chapter 28

The Holy Spirit and the Cross

The Holy Spirit always leads us to the cross. It was so with Christ. The Spirit taught Him and enabled Him to offer himself without spot to God.

It was so with the disciples. The Spirit, with whom they were filled, led them to preach Christ as the Crucified One. Later on He led them to glory in the fellowship of the cross, by which they were deemed worthy to suffer for Christ's sake.

The cross directed them again to the Spirit. When Christ had borne the cross, He received the Spirit from the Father that He might be poured out. When the three thousand newly converted, mentioned in the book of Acts, bowed before the Crucified One, they received the promise of the Holy Spirit. When the disciples rejoiced in their experience of the fellowship of the cross, they received the Holy Spirit afresh. The union between the Spirit and the cross is indissoluble; they belong inseparably to one another. We see this especially in the epistles of Paul: "Before your very eyes Jesus Christ was clearly portrayed as crucified. I would like to learn just one thing from you: Did you receive the Spirit by observing the law, or by believing what you heard?" (Galatians 3:1–2).

"Christ redeemed us from the curse of the law by becoming a curse for us, for it is written: 'Cursed is everyone who is hung on a tree.' He redeemed us in order that the blessing given to Abraham might come to the Gentiles" (Galatians 3:13–14).

"God sent his Son, born of a woman, born under law, to redeem those under law, that we might receive the full rights of sons. Because you are sons, God sent the Spirit of his Son into our hearts, the Spirit who calls out, '*Abba,* Father'" (Galatians 4:4–6).

"Those who belong to Christ Jesus have crucified the sinful nature with its passions and desires. Since we live by the Spirit, let us keep in step with the Spirit" (Galatians 5:24–25).

"You also died to the law through the body of Christ . . . that we [may] serve in the new way of the Spirit, and not in the old way of the written code" (Romans 7:4–6).

"Because through Christ Jesus the law of the Spirit of life set me free from the law of sin and death. For what the law was powerless to do in that it was weakened by the sinful nature, God did by sending his own Son in the likeness of sinful man to be a sin offering. And so he condemned sin in sinful man, in order that the righteous requirements of the law might be fully met in us, who do not live according to the sinful nature but according to the Spirit" (Romans 8:2–4).

Always, in everything, the Spirit and the cross are inseparable—even in heaven: "Then I saw a Lamb, looking as if it had been slain, standing in the center of the throne, encircled by the four living creatures and the elders. He had seven horns and seven eyes, which are the seven spirits of God sent out into all the earth" (Revelation 5:6).

"Then the angel showed me the river of the water of life, [is this the Holy Spirit?] as clear as crystal, flowing from the throne of God and of the Lamb" (Revelation 22:1; author's bracketed note). When Moses smote the rock, the water streamed out, and Israel drank of it. When the Rock Christ was smitten, and He had taken His place as the slain Lamb on the throne of God, there flowed out from under the throne the fullness of the Holy Spirit for the whole world.

How foolish it is to pray for the fullness of the Spirit if we have not first placed ourselves under the full power of the cross! Just think of the one hundred and twenty disciples. The crucifixion of Christ had touched, broken, and taken possession of their hearts. They could speak or think of nothing else, and when the Crucified One had shown them His hands and His feet, He said to them, "Receive the Holy Spirit." And so also, with their hearts full of the crucified Christ, now received up into heaven, they were prepared to be filled with the Spirit. They dared to proclaim to the people: "Repent and believe in the Crucified One"; and they also received the Holy Spirit.

Christ yielded himself unreservedly to the cross. It was the will of His Father. It was the only way to redeem the lost. Integral to the act of self-sacrifice and death was a disposition borne in Him by the Spirit—a disposition that would be imparted to His disciples and to all who put their trust in Him. The cross demands our entire life. To comply with this demand requires nothing less than an act of the will, and for this we are unfit in the natural sense. But if we submit our will to Him who stands waiting to receive us, we will be enabled to do what we could not otherwise do.

Chapter 29

The Cross in Contrast to the Flesh and the World

The cross and the flesh are deadly enemies. The cross would condemn and put to death the flesh. The flesh desires to cast aside and conquer the cross. Many, as they hear of the cross as the indispensable preparation for the fullness of the Holy Spirit, will find out what there is in them that must yet be crucified. We are to understand that our entire nature is sentenced to death, and we must die, by the cross, so that the new life in Christ may rule in us. Let us gain such an insight into the fallen condition of our nature and its enmity against God that we become not only willing but anxious to be wholly freed from it.

We must learn to say with Paul: "In me, that is in my flesh, there dwells no good thing. The mind of the flesh is enmity against God: it is not subject to the law of God, neither indeed can be." The very essence of the flesh is to hate God and His holy law. The wonder of redemption is that Christ has borne on the cross the judgment and curse of God on the flesh and has forever nailed it to the cursed tree. If a man only believes God's Word about this mind of the flesh, and then longs to be delivered from it, he learns to love the cross as his deliverer from the power of the Enemy.

Our old man—our former nature—is crucified with Christ, and our one hope is to receive this by faith and to hold it fast. "They that are Christ's have crucified the flesh." They have willingly declared that they will daily regard the flesh that is in them as the enemy of God, the enemy of Christ, and the enemy of their soul's salvation. They will treat it as having received its deserved reward in being nailed to the cross.

This is a part of the eternal redemption Christ has brought to us. It is not something we can grasp with our understanding or accomplish through our own strength. It is something the Lord Jesus himself will give us if we are willing to abide in His fellowship day by day and to receive everything from Him. It is something the Holy Spirit will teach us, and He will impart it to us as an experience. He will show how He can give victory in the power of the cross over all that is of the flesh.

What the flesh is in the small circle of my own person, so the world is in the larger circle of humankind. The flesh and the world are two manifestations of the same "god of this world," who is served by both. When the cross deals with the flesh as cursed, we at once discover what the nature and the power of the world are: "They hated both me and my Father." The proof of this was that they crucified Christ. But Christ obtained the victory on the cross and freed us from the power of the world. Now we can say with Paul: "May I never boast except in the cross of our Lord Jesus Christ, through which the world has been crucified to me, and I to the world" (Galatians 6:14).

Every day the cross was to Paul a holy reality, both in

what he had to suffer from the world and in the victory the cross continually gave Him. John wrote: "We know that we are children of God, and that the whole world is under the control of the evil one" (1 John 5:19). "Who is it that overcomes the world? Only he who believes that Jesus is the Son of God. This is the one who came by water and blood—Jesus Christ. He did not come by water only, but by water and blood. And it is the Spirit who testifies, because the Spirit is the truth" (1 John 5:5–6). Against the two great powers of the god of this world, God has given us two great powers from heaven: the cross and the Holy Spirit.

Chapter 30

The Spirit and the Cross

Do you ever wonder why there are not more men and women who can witness, with joyful hearts, that the Spirit of God has taken possession of them and given them new power to witness? Another heart-searching question is more urgent: What is it that hinders us? The Father in heaven is more willing than an earthly father to give bread to his child, and yet the cry arises: "Is the Spirit restricted or hampered? Is this His work?"

Some will acknowledge that the hindrance undoubtedly lies in the fact that the church is under the sway of the flesh and the world. They understand too little of the heart-changing power of the cross of Christ. Because of this, the Spirit does not have vessels into which He can pour His fullness.

Many complain that the subject is too high or too deep. It proves how little we have appropriated and put into practice the teaching of Paul and of Christ about the cross. I bring you a message of joy. The Spirit who is in you, in however limited a measure, is prepared to bring you under His teaching, to lead you to the cross, and by His heavenly instruction to make you aware of what the crucified Christ wants to do for you and in you.

Take time, so that He may reveal the heavenly mystery to

you. He will show you how the neglect of private prayer has hindered your fellowship with Christ; He will reveal the cross to you and the powerful operation of the Spirit. He will teach you what is meant by self-denial, taking up your cross daily, and losing your life in order to follow Him.

In spite of your having acknowledged your ignorance, your lack of spiritual insight and fellowship with the cross, He is willing to teach you and to make known to you the secret of a spiritual life beyond all your expectations.

Begin at the beginning. Be faithful in private prayer. Thank Him that you can count on Him to meet you there. Even though everything may appear cold and dark, bow in silence before the loving Lord Jesus, who so longs for you. Thank the Father that He has given you the Spirit. Be assured that all you do not know and still need to learn about the flesh, the world, and the cross—the Spirit of Christ will make known to you. Only believe that this blessing is for you. Christ belongs to you, and He longs to obtain full possession of you through the Holy Spirit. But for this to happen, time and faith is necessary. Give Him time in prayer every day. You can be sure that He will fulfill His promise in you.

Our identity is in the way we love and serve one another: "Anyone who claims to be in the light but hates his brother is still in the darkness. Whoever loves his brother lives in the light, and there is nothing in him to make him stumble. But whoever hates his brother is in the darkness and walks around in the darkness; he does not know where he is going, because the darkness has blinded him. I write to you, dear children, because your sins have been forgiven on account of his name. I write to you, fathers, because you have known him who is from the beginning. I write to you, young men, because you have overcome the evil one. I write to you, dear children, because you have known the Father. I write to you, fathers, because you have known him who is from the beginning. I write to you, young men, because you are strong, and the word of God lives in you, and you have overcome the evil one. Do not love the world or anything in the world. If anyone loves the world, the love of the Father is not in him" (1 John 2:9–15).

Persevere—in addition to all that you ask for yourself—in prayer for your congregation, your church, your minister; for all believers; for the whole church of God, that God may strengthen them by the power of His Spirit, so that Christ may dwell in their hearts by faith. What a blessed time it will be when the answer comes! Continue in prayer. The Spirit will reveal and glorify Christ and His cross, the Lamb who was slain, standing in the center of the throne (Revelation 5:6).

Chapter 31

Christ, Our Example

Our Head, Christ, took the lowest place on the cross, and so He has marked out for us, His members, the lowest place. The radiance of God's glory (Hebrews 1:3) became the afflicted One of men (Isaiah 53:4). Since that time the only right we have is to be the last and the lowest. When we claim anything more, we have not yet fully understood the cross.

We seek for a higher life, and we will find it if we go deeper into the fellowship of the cross with our Lord. God has given the Crucified One the highest place (Revelation 5). Shall we not give Him the same place? We do this when from moment to moment we conduct ourselves as those who are crucified with Him (Galatians 2:19–20). In this way we honor the Lord who suffered for us.

We long for full victory. And we find it as we more fully enter into the fellowship of His cross. The Lamb obtained His greatest victory with His hands and feet nailed to the cross. We abide in the shadow of the Almighty only so long as we abide under the shadow of the cross. The cross must be our home. There alone are we sheltered and protected. We first understand our own cross when we have understood His. May we desire to get so close to it that we not only see it but we also embrace it, take it up, and make it our own.

Then the cross asserts itself in us, and we experience His power—to the point that we do not faint under it but carry it with joy.

What would Jesus be without His cross? His pierced feet have bruised the head of the Enemy, and His pierced hands have spoiled the devil's tactics completely (Matthew 12:29). What are we without the cross? Do not let the cross go, but hold it securely. Do we think we can go by any other road than that which the Master trod? Many of us will make no progress until we take up the cross of humility and self-denial.

Epilogue

Allow me a final word to the reader regarding the disposition of mind to which this book appeals.

It is not enough that one should understand and appropriate the thought of the writer and then rejoice because of the new insight he has obtained and the pleasure the knowledge has brought. There is something else that is of great importance. I must surrender myself to the truth, so that I will be ready with an undivided will to immediately perform all that I learn to be God's will.

In a book such as this, dealing with the life of prayer and intimate fellowship with God, it is indispensable that we should be prepared to receive and obey all that we see to be according to the Word and will of God. Where this disposition to receive and obey is lacking, knowledge only serves to make the heart less capable of receiving a fuller life. Satan endeavors to become the master of the Christian's prayer time. This is because he knows that the testimony of the one who has been unfaithful in prayer will cause little damage to his kingdom. Spiritual power to lead the lost to the Lord, or to build up the children of God, simply will not flow from a prayerless life. This power comes only through persevering prayer.

The great question is: Shall we earnestly set ourselves to win back again the weapon of believing prayer that Satan has, at least in a measure, taken away from us? Let us set before ourselves the serious importance of this conflict. As far as each minister is concerned, everything depends on whether or not he is a man of prayer—one who in the inner room is clothed each day with power from on high. We, in common with the church throughout the whole world, must acknowledge that prayer does not have the place in our service of God that it ought to have.

The public consecration that many believers have made at conferences, crusades, and other meetings, is not an easy thing. And even when the step is taken, old habits and the power of the flesh will tend to nullify it. The power of faith is not yet alive and well. It will cost us great effort and great sacrifice to conquer the devil in this area in the name of Christ. Our churches are the battlefields in which Satan will muster all his power to prevent us from becoming people of prayer. So much depends on this for our congregations, God's kingdom, and for us as individuals.

With fear and trembling and much prayer, I have written what I trust will help to encourage Christians in this conflict. With a feeling of deep unworthiness, I venture to offer myself as a guide to the place of prayer—which is the way to holiness and to true fellowship with God.

I have asked the Lord to give this book a place in the prayer rooms of many, and that He would assist the reader, when he sees God's will, to immediately yield himself to do it. In war, everything depends on each soldier's being obedient to the word of command, even though it might cost him his life. In our struggle with the wiles of Satan, we will not conquer unless each one of us stands ready to say from the heart: "What God says, I will do; if I see that anything is according to His will, I will immediately receive it and act upon it."

Epilogue

May there be in each one of us a spirit of surrender to immediate obedience to all we read here that is in accord with the Word of God.

God grant that by His great grace this book may prove a bond of fellowship by which we may think of one another, help each other, and strengthen everyone we know for the conflict in prayer by which the Enemy of our souls may be overcome and the life of God be gloriously realized!